BALANCING THE FEDERAL BUDGET
The Cure for U.S. Wealth Dissipation

BALANCING THE FEDERAL BUDGET
The Cure for U.S. Wealth Dissipation
Ernest J. Oppenheimer, Ph.D.

Pen & Podium, Inc.

Balancing the Federal Budget
By Ernest J. Oppenheimer, Ph.D.

© Copyright 1990 by Ernest J. Oppenheimer

Publisher: Pen & Podium, Inc.
       40 Central Park South
       New York, N.Y. 10019
       (212) 759-8454

10 9 8 7 6 5 4 3 2 1

Printed in the United States of America

ISBN-0-9603982-6-0

Library of Congress Catalog Card No. 90-62918

Books by Ernest J. Oppenheimer, Ph.D.

Balancing the Federal Budget
Natural Gas, the Best Energy Choice
Gasoline Tax Advantages
Solving the U.S. Energy Problem
Natural Gas, the New Energy Leader
A Realistic Approach to U.S. Energy Independence
The Inflation Swindle

Contents

Foreword

By William R. Grant, Chairman of Galen Partners, a venture capital firm, and a director of five New York Stock Exchange companies. Formerly, he was president of a major investment banking firm and chairman of a large money management organization.

When I first met Ernest Oppenheimer many years ago, he was doing research on investments. His work was characterized by innovative thinking, thorough research, a willingness to challenge conventional ideas, and persistence. Equally important, his investment recommendations were usually highly profitable.

In recent years, Dr. Oppenheimer has applied himself to finding solutions to such national problems as inflation, energy policy, and the federal budget. The same qualities that helped him discover outstanding investments have been utilized for the benefit of the nation. His pioneering work on the gasoline tax is worthy of particular mention. He probably knows more about the gasoline tax than anybody else in the country. Our leaders in government would be well advised to make use of his expertise on this topic, which can play a key role in helping to solve many of our problems.

In the book on the federal budget, Dr. Oppenheimer looks at the underlying realities that have caused deficit spending to become increasingly ineffectual in stimulating the economy. He reaches the conclusion that for the past sixty years our government has been acting on wrong assumptions about the supposed benefits from deficit spending. Far from being a panacea for dealing with economic issues, deficit spending is the main cause of our predicament and has led to the massive dissipation of wealth. The author excels in making a case for contrary thinking on budget issues.

The second half of the book is devoted to solutions for the budget predicament. The author shows that the best approach

11

is to eliminate the real operating budget deficit (which is more than twice as large as the reported deficit) and, in fact, to generate budget surpluses on a sustained basis. In addition to solving the government's financial problems, this policy would create the conditions for minimizing inflation, lowering interest rates to levels not seen in decades, and for restoring wealth creation to its rightful place in our free enterprise economy. The book is a strong affirmation of classical economic thinking in relation to budget policies. While Dr. Oppenheimer is non-partisan, his solution is compatible with the traditional position of the Republican Party.

The book is easy to understand and holds the reader's interest. I particularly liked the author's imagined interviews with a Democrat and a Republican at the end of each chapter. While these interviews are fictional, they convey a great many practical insights into the budget process. The technique combines education with entertainment, which enhances the effectiveness of the book's power to communicate.

Dr. Oppenheimer's work makes a major contribution to understanding the budget predicament and how to solve it. For the sake of the nation, I hope this book will be widely read by those who are concerned with the future of our country, including our leaders.

Preface

During the past sixty years, the U.S. government has relied on deficit spending to stimulate the economy in times of recession. In the past decade, *unprecedented deficits were incurred while the economy was growing.* The real operating budget deficit* was running at an annual rate of $350 billion *prior to the onset of the 1990 recession.* It seems unlikely that even higher budget deficits would provide sufficient stimulation to move the nation out of the recession on a sustained basis. In fact, additional deficits might prove to be counterproductive.

My studies indicate that the deficit spending approach is fundamentally flawed. It is an irresponsible way of dealing with the nation's financial affairs. It has led to massive wealth dissipation and to the implementation of policies that are harmful to the national interest. The best solution to this predicament is a return to financial orthodoxy, which would require decisive steps to balance the budget.

Such action is all the more desirable in view of the fact that our budget policies have unwittingly enriched foreigners at the expense of the American people (see pages 69-87). This reality is particularly evident in relation to defense spending and gasoline taxes.

Ever since the outbreak of the Second World War, the U.S. has subsidized its allies with an enormously costly defense umbrella. We have continued this policy even though our financial resources have become seriously depleted while those of our allies have grown substantially. Currently, the U.S. devotes about $300 billion annually, or six percent of its gross national product (GNP), to defense. Our European allies spend about three percent of their GNP for this purpose, while the Japanese dedicate only one percent of their GNP to this task. These differences in defense spending play a major role in causing our wealth to decline while enriching our allies. For the "priv-

---

*The real operating budget deficit includes the following: (1) The deficit as reported by the government; (2) The cost of the savings and loan bailout; and (3) Trust fund surpluses for Social Security and other programs that should be excluded from federal revenues.

ilege" of defending foreign nations, we load ourselves down with huge amounts of debt and sell our assets to the beneficiaries of our largess at bargain prices. This self-destructive behavior poses a grave threat to the national interest.

To cope with this dangerous situation, we should make it a cardinal principle that those allies who are our creditors and/or who enjoy a trade surplus with us should pay in full for any defense services we render them. Moreover, we should make sharp cuts in defense spending to take advantage of improved relations with the Soviet Union. See pages 91-103 and 169-170 for more information.

All other industrial nations have learned from experience that the best way for coping with the energy problem is through high taxes on gasoline. Such taxes average $2 per gallon in Western Europe and the Far East. In contrast, gasoline taxes in the U.S. average thirty-five cents per gallon, of which the federal government collects fourteen cents. Our low gasoline tax policy benefits foreign oil producers at the expense of U.S. consumers. A substantial gasoline tax increase would make a major contribution to reducing the federal budget deficit, strengthening energy security, and improving the economy. Pages 105-124 and 167-169 elaborate on this topic.

A continuation of present budget policies would endanger the government's solvency, undermine the financial foundation for democracy, jeopardize private wealth, and compromise our independence. A balanced budget is the best antidote for this malaise. Moreover, the implementation of responsible budget policies would provide the private sector with the conditions, notably low interest and inflation rates on a sustained basis, to move the economy forward. Productive investments in the private sector would replace wasteful government spending as the engines for economic growth. Pages 128-161 provide specific information for accomplishing these goals.

As informed citizenry is essential to meet the challenges confronting the nation. This book is dedicated to the task of helping readers understand the budget problem and related issues, to enable them to play a constructive role in supporting correct policies.

PART I. THE PROBLEM:
BUDGET DEFICITS
AND WEALTH DISSIPATION

Chapter 1
Introduction

I have been actively involved in studying budget matters ever since I wrote the book *The Inflation Swindle,* which was published in 1977. In connection with that project, I consulted classical sources, including *The Wealth of Nations,* by Adam Smith. This book presented the viewpoint that governments heavily in debt invariably manipulated the currency in their favor and defrauded their creditors. It called this procedure "a disguised form of bankruptcy." Smith cited historical examples which illustrated that this process can make the currency worthless and may lead to the collapse of the nation. To avoid this danger, Smith took the position that governments should live within their means and should not be allowed to accumulate debt.

My next five books dealt with the energy problem, which has played a key role in contributing to budget deficits since 1973. The oil price escalations of the 1970's caused inflationary pressures, high interest rates, foreign trade imbalances, and the loss of wealth to foreign oil producers. One of my recommendations for coping with this predicament was to increase the gasoline tax by $1 per gallon. My book *Gasoline Tax Advantages,* published in 1987, elaborated on this thesis.

Between 1984 and 1988, I wrote more than fifty letters to President Reagan and members of his Cabinet. In these letters

17

I recommended actions to reduce the budget deficits by combining a gasoline tax increase with substantial spending cuts. I continued the process of communicating my views to President Bush and members of his Administration. Altogether, these letters would fill a sizeable book.

The persistence of unprecedented budget deficits and the accompanying foreign trade deficits and loss of U.S. assets to foreigners during the Reagan era heightened my concern that the nation was engaged in self-destructive behavior. I recalled Adam Smith's warnings about the risks to all wealth and to the integrity of society from these policies. I tried my best to alert the Reagan Administration to these dangers, but my efforts were in vain. It was evident that President Reagan and his Cabinet had no interest in views that disagreed with their policies.

In my work as a social scientist, I have long been interested in investigating the role of irrational behavior in human affairs. This phenomenon is well known in individuals, who often engage in actions that are against their own best self interest. While we know from experience that groups, including nations, also can act irrationally, the process is less well understood. I have made some discoveries which can shed light on this subject and which can be useful in dealing with the budget predicament.

My studies indicate that irrational behavior can be understood by investigating assumptions. Chronically wrong assumptions lead to persistent negative consequences. For example, if government policies continue to produce huge deficits in spite of the professed intention to balance the budget, there must be something wrong with the assumptions underlying those policies. Similarly, policies that may have been realistic under one set of circumstances may become counterproductive in a different context. Defense spending may serve as an illustration. At the end of the Second World War, the U.S. was the only power in the Free World which had the resources to defend Western Europe and Japan from Soviet aggression. It was appropriate under those circumstances that the U.S.

should carry the lion's share of the costs involved in providing for the common defense. However, under present circumstances, when our allies are affluent and can pay for their own defense, it makes no sense to subsidize them with our defense umbrella and undermine our finances in the process.

I have utilized the study of assumptions wherever it seemed relevant in the preparation of this book. It has been helpful in understanding harmful consequences from chronic deficit spending. It has facilitated clarifying the difficulties involved in implementing a gasoline tax increase, even though such a policy would be most beneficial to the American people. It has also served a useful purpose in understanding the dynamics of ideological dogmatism, which has played such an important role in the budget policies of the Reagan Administration.

Ideological dogmatism interferes with rational budget behavior. People whose actions are dominated by such an approach have simplistic notions, rigid attitudes, and an uncompromising orientation. They invariably have hidden motivations and exploitative objectives. They tend to blame their adversaries for their own misdeeds. Their behavior is undemocratic and inimical to realistic budget procedures. The massive wealth dissipation that occurred during the Reagan era was largely caused by the dominance of ideological dogmatism over realistic behavior.

In a democratic society, budget issues are normally decided through a process of compromise among major participants. To understand the budget process, it is important to know the premises of the key players. In our society, Republicans and Democrats are the main determinants of budget policies. While there are a great many points of view by members of any given political party, there is a broad consensus of Democrats that differs from the consensus of Republicans.

As an approximate guideline, it is assumed that most Democrats advocate policies that favor the middle class and the poor over the rich. In line with this orientation, they want more taxes on the rich and fewer on their own constituents.

19

They also want more spending on programs that favor their supporters. Most Democrats would support actions to reduce the budget deficit, but they want to make sure that their constituents don't pay a disproportionate price to achieve this goal.

Businessmen and the wealthy are the core constituents of the Republican Party. Most Republicans don't like progressive taxes, which they consider an unfair burden. Similarly, they want to keep social spending under control, lest it lead to inceased taxes. Historically, a balanced budget had top priority for Republicans, who shared the concerns expressed by Adam Smith and other classical writers on economics about the harmful consequences to private wealth from public debt. This dedication to a balanced budget was largely absent during the Reagan era. However, it seems likely that President Bush would like to restore this tradition.

To give the reader an appreciation of how Democrats and Republicans might view key elements of the budget, I have followed the procedure of presenting imagined interviews with party representatives after my exposition on the topic. It should be emphasized that the views expressed are based on my own judgment and are not necessarily accurate reflections of the thinking of actual Democrats or Republicans.

An Overview of Wealth Dissipation

When a nation lives chronically beyond its means, it dissipates wealth to pay for its profligacy. Real operating budget deficits and the net sale of assets to foreigners are the chief components of wealth dissipation. During the past decade, the wealth dissipation process has reached an alarming level, which jeopardizes the financial, economic, and political foundation of the nation. Unsound budget policies are primarily responsible for this predicament.

The federal budget is closely linked to politics. Both major political parties try to utilize the budget to gain popularity with voters. As a general rule, politicians will support budget policies that appeal to their constituents and oppose those that do not. If there is a conflict between getting elected and solving the budget problem, the political choice will invariably be in favor of election. Fundamental solutions to the budget problem will involve choices that would not be immediately popular with voters. This reality interferes with proper approaches to solving the budget problem. It is unlikely that the normal political process will lead to a resolution of the budget predicament unless the voters are made aware of the crisis facing the nation.

Deficit spending, which is at the heart of the budget problem, has great appeal to politicians of both political parties. This procedure makes it possible to increase spending without raising taxes. Moreover, it stimulates the economy, at least for a while. While these benefits are very visible and concrete, the costs tend to be hidden and abstract. Higher inflation and interest rates, and the escalating national debt, are the major costs of this insidious policy. The fact that the latter has grown to more than $3,000 billion is proof of the great political appeal of deficit spending.

Economic realities have a way of spoiling the games politicians like to play. With the passage of time and the accumulations of ever larger amounts of debt, the benefits become smaller and the harmful consequences more visible. The artificial stimulation of the economy has led to excessive spending by the private sector and to inadequate domestic savings to pay for the deficits. As a result, large foreign trade imbalances and heavy dependence on foreign sources of capital have accompanied the budget deficits. Like deficit spending, the loss of assets to foreigners has the visible effect of stimulating the economy, but it involves the hidden cost of adding to the wealth dissipation and undermining the nation's independence.

The process of wealth dissipation has become increasingly menacing to the nation's vital interests. During the period 1981-1990, the U.S. has accumulated about $2,300 billion real operating budget deficits and has sold $700 billion net assets to foreigners. It is estimated that in 1991 the real operating budget deficit will be $380 billion and the net loss of U.S. assets to foreigners will total about $50 billion. Altogether, the nation will dissipate $430 billion of its wealth in a year that is unlikely to show much, if any, economic growth. Our wealth dissipation is increasingly ineffectual in stimulating the economy, and may in fact not be able to ward off a recession.

Politicians of both political parties are in a quandary. If they do nothing, the chances are strong that the nation will experience depressed economic conditions that might degenerate into a major financial and economic crisis. Adding even more to the deficit spending spree is hardly a viable option. To reduce the budget deficit seems to be the only feasible procedure. However, in their view this option entails the risk of precipitating the very recession they are trying to avoid.

To cope with this predicament, the politicians have decided to define the problem in a manner that is more susceptible to solution than the real operating deficit. Their deficit reduction negotiations revolve around the estimated *reported deficit* of $169 billion for 1969. This figure excludes the cost of the savings and loan bailout, which is estimated at $62 billion. Similarly, the government will count trust fund surpluses from Social Security and other programs it administers as "federal revenues," even though these funds belong to the participants in those programs, not to the federal government. The amounts involved total an estimated $150 billion.

Even this artificially constructed deficit reduction program has encountered major obstacles. The program would apparently involve reducing the deficit by about $50 billion in 1991. Half of this sum would consist of broadly based spending cuts and half of tax increases. Most Republicans in the Congress have already declared their opposition to any tax increases. The Democrats want to cut more on defense and less on social programs than the Republicans. Almost all participants in the negotiations are worried that a $50 billion deficit reduction package might make conditions worse for the already weak economy. It is likely that they will include a provision in any agreement that would cancel the program in case a recession took place.

To place this matter into perspective, the $50 billion deficit reduction is only a pittance in relation to the gross national product in excess of $5,000 billion. The economic forces at play may swamp the deficit reduction program like an ocean tide washing over a weakly built barrier.

The solution to the budget predicament and related issues is not likely to emerge from the deficit reduction discussions currently underway in Washington. My own studies have led to a quite different approach. We should eliminate the real operating budget deficit of $380 billion as soon as possible and start generating a budget surplus. By making appropriate choices of spending cuts and tax increases, we can also lay the basis for creating foreign trade surpluses and eliminating dependence on foreign capital to finance our deficits. Theses actions would transform wealth dissipation into wealth creation and accumulation. As a result, interest rates would drop sharply, capital investments would boom, and the Federal Reserve would have freedom to guide the economy in a desirable fashion. The specific terms of this package, which are spelled out in the concluding chapter of this book as "Option 3," also involve a special procedure to ridding the nation of the festering financial and political wounds left in the wake of the savings and loan fiasco.

This package should be implemented as soon as possible, regardless of the general economic situation. It is our best hope for infusing new life into the economy. If we get into a recession, this approach will enable us to cope with it more effectively than the other alternatives. The transformation from wealth dissipation to wealth accumulation is our best choice for overcoming the malaise currently afflicting the nation.

This proposal involves the mobilization of the American people on their own behalf. By properly employing their financial and economic resources, they can solve the budget deficit problem and related issues. The elimination of heavy dependence on foreign capital will be a valuable byproduct of this approach. As will be shown in Chapter 4, the massive transfer of U.S. wealth to foreigners in recent years was caused primarily by the defense spending spree during the Reagan era. Our defense spending policies were anachronistic even before Reagan, but they became much more so after he doubled expenditures for this purpose. The defense buildup constituted an enormous drain on our financial resources, while subsidizing our affluent allies. In effect, for the "privilege" of defending their territory from possible agression, we dissipated our wealth and were grateful for their willingness to lend us funds and to acquire our assets at bargain prices. In fairness to our allies, it should be noted that they did not ask us to double defense spending. The Reagan Administration undertook this policy on its own initiative. In any case, the time is long overdue for correcting this self-destructive behavior. Cuts in defense spending would make a major contribution to reducing budget and foreign trade deficits, thereby improving the conditions for safeguarding the nation's wealth.

We can no longer afford to dissipate our wealth on the basis of politics, ideology, or just plain ignorance. It is hoped that this book will provide the insights with which we can solve the budget deficit problem and transform our nation from self-destructive wealth dissipating policies to ones that create wealth and restore soundness to our affairs.

Budget Misconceptions

The reader should be alerted to the fact that many conventional ideas about the budget are simplistic, deceptive, or erroneous. A brief summary of such budget misconceptions at the beginning of the book may be useful in facilitating a more realistic perspective. The misconceptions are italicized; they are followed by clarifying comments.

1. Budget deficits are necessary to stimulate the economy. This misconception can be traced ot the New Deal policies of the 1930's and the writings of John Maynard Keynes, the British economist, of the same era. In fairness to Keynes, it should be noted that he did not advocate chronic deficit spending. He recommended it only for times when the economy was depressed. In actuality, the economy can do just fine without deficit spending. In fact, one can make a strong case for the position that most of the time deficit spending is counterproductive. It leads to misallocation of resources, undermines the government's finances, and jeopardizes the wealth of the private sector.

2. In view of current weakness in the economy, deficit reduction should be postponed. Realistic measures for reducing budget deficits, such as sharp cuts in defense spending and increased taxes on gasoline and on luxuries, should be implemented whether the economy is weak or strong. These actions will set the stage for significantly lower interest rates, which will release forces in the private sector that will counteract recessionary trends. It should be remembered that the less money is borrowed by the goveernment, the more is available to the private sector at attractive rates.

3. Drastic cuts in defense spending might precipitate a recession. This misconception is a variation on the theme discussed above. If the funds saved from defense spending cuts are applied to deficit reduction, the previously cited positive consequences on interest rates will ensue. Moreover, a substantial part of the defense spending cuts should take place overseas, which would yield the additional benefit of helping our foreign trade balance.

4. Deficits should be reduced solely through spending cuts on social programs. This notion was a central theme of the Reagan wing of the Republican Party. The record during the Reagan era has shown that this approach is unsound and unworkable politically. Its primary purpose was to deceive the public about the main cause of the deficits, namely the huge defense buildup, combined with the unwillingness to pay for it with increased taxes.

5. *Economic growth will provide sufficient government revenue increases to eliminate the deficits.* The economy experienced strong growth between 1983 and 1989, but the government's real operating budget deficit did not decline and is currently at record levels. To continue adhering to this fallacious notion in the face of such experience is irresponsible behavior. Wishful thinking about economic growth should not be used as a substitute for realistic actions, including spending cuts and tax increases.

6. *All tax increases are bad because they take money from the private sector and encourage wasteful spending by politicians.* This simplistic notion is another central feature of the Reagan ideology. In actuality, if tax increases are dedicated to deficit reduction, they serve an essential function. Moreover, carefully selected taxes can accomplish several goals at the same time. For example, an increase in the gasoline tax would strengthen energy security, improve the foreign trade balance, help the environment, and raise substantial revenues for the government. My studies indicate that each dollar of gasoline tax would generate several dollars of benefits. It is an ideal tax for helping to achieve the goal of transforming our economy from wealth dissipation to wealth creation.

7. *Weakening the government's finances is good for the private sector.* Nothing could be further from the truth. The precarious position of the government's finances is the most troublesome aspect of the present predicament. All private wealth is placed in jeopardy when the government is loaded down with heavy debts and chronically high budget deficits. Classical economic theory holds that the government should not be allowed to get into debt, lest it implement policies that defraud its creditors and undermine the currency by means of inflation. We should make a determined effort to stop budget deficits and to start repaying the outstanding government debt.

8. Foreign acquisition of U.S. assets is healthy because it stimulates the economy. Under the circumstances that have prevailed during the past decade, foreign acquisition of U.S. assets was an integral part of the wealth dissipation process. It was very harmful to our long-term interests. We loaded ourselves down with obligations to foreigners for which we will have to pay for decades to come. In the process, we undermined our financial, economic, and political independence. These dangerous consequences are all the more unconscionable when one considers the fact that the largest single cause of this wealth transfer was our asinine policy of subsidizing affluent allies with our excessive defense spending.

9. A lower value for the dollar will improve our international trade and help the budget. A lower dollar increases inflationary pressures, which cause interest rates to rise. Both of these factors have harmful consequences for the budget. Moreover, high interest rates increase costs of exporters, which has adverse effects on our competitive position in the international marketplace. Last but not least, the low dollar makes it easier for foreigners to acquire U.S. assets at bargain prices. It is a major contributor to the wealth dissipation process. We should take decisive actions to balance the federal budget, which would strengthen the dollar and help solve all of our other financial and economic problems.

10. Democracy requires that special interests and partisan politics should play a predominant role in the budget process. If democracy is survive, the national interest has to be placed ahead of all other considerations. Special interests and partisan politics in relation to the budget process have done great harm to the government's finances. The ideological tactics of the Reagan Adminstration were particularly pernicious and played a key role in causing the most massive wealth dissipation in history.

Chapter 2
The High Cost of Deficit Spending

Ever since the 1930's, the federal government has been addicted to deficit spending to stimulate economic activity. This approach gives the misleading impression of getting something for nothing, when in actuality it dissipates the nation's wealth and jeopardizes its vital interests. Classical economic theory rejects the notion that deficit spending is a valid procedure for stimulating economic growth.

The theoretical formulation for deficit spending was provided by the British economist John Maynard Keynes. He presented the thesis that in times of depressed economic activity, the government's expenditures should exceed its revenues. This policy should be accompanied by measures to facilitate the availability of credit at low interest rates. Keynes also emphasized that at times of strong economic activity, the government should generate surpluses and retire the debt that was incurred during the depression. Keynes did not advocate deficit spending as a substitute for financial discipline, nor did he recommend such action as a replacement for realistic measures to cope with challenges other than economic depressions. Most of the deficit spending that has occurred during the past sixty years cannot be justified on the basis of Keynesian theory.

The Roosevelt Administration utilized deficit spending and easy credit policy to deal with the depression of the 1930's. Since that time, the federal government has incurred budget deficits in all but six years. The last budget surplus was achieved in 1969. During the period 1933 to 1990, deficits totaled about $3,000 billion, while budget surpluses aggregated $30 billion, a ratio of one hundred to one. Politicians ignored what Keynes had written about the necessity to accumulate budget surpluses during times of strong economic activity. Moreover, deficits were used for purposes that Keynes never intended. For example, the government relied on deficit spending to cope with the oil price escalations of the 1970's and for the defense buildup of the 1980's. In practical terms, deficit spending has become a substitute for responsible behavior by the government.

The political appeal of deficit spending can be explained by the fact that the benefits are highly visible, while the costs tend to be hidden. Increased government spending and/or reduced taxes, which are the basic causes of deficits, tend to stimulate economic growth and make politicians popular with voters.

While the costs of deficit spending may be hidden, they are very real. The mushrooming federal debt is the most obvious cost. This debt has grown from almost nothing in 1933 to about $3,000 billion in 1990. As the debt increases, an ever larger share of federal revenues has to be devoted to interest payments. Moreover, heavy government borrowing requirements tend to put upward pressure on interest rates, which has negative consequences for the economy. Inflation almost invariably accompanies deficit spending, particularly if it takes place at a time of strong economic activity. Chronically high budget deficits tend to generate foreign trade deficits, a weakened currency, and the loss of assets of foreigners. In the later stages of chronic deficit spending, the negative factors far outweigh the economic growth benefits.

Deficit spending was first embraced by the Democrats in the 1930's and has been popular with them ever since. However, they generally tried to keep deficits from getting out of hand; annual deficits did not exceed $60 billion even at the peak of spending during the Second World War. The Republicans opposed deficit spending until President Nixon openly embraced such a policy. New converts to a seductive cause often go to extremes. President Ford was first in reaching the $100 billion deficit mark. He was easily overshadowed by the Reagan Administration, which generated more budget deficits than all previous presidencies put together.

Chronic deficit spending has many attributes characteristic of irrational behavior. Harmful effects are ignored or rationalized as being beneficial. For example, high interest rates are blamed on the Federal Reserve rather than on the government's irresponsible behavior. The loss of assets to foreigners is rationalized as being a positive indication, for it shows that foreigners consider the U.S. an attractive place to invest. Wishful thinking about closing the budget deficit through economic growth is used as an excuse for opposing realistic actions, such as spending cuts and/or tax increases. A variation on this theme is to blame the deficits on the other political party for not cutting programs that benefit their constituencies. To maintain the myth of an eventual budget balance without doing anything concrete to achieve it, politicians embrace symbolic gestures that supposedly will assure positive results, such as long-term budget balancing plans, which invariably fail to achieve their objective, or constitutional reforms that prohibit deficits to their successors. As deficit spending becomes institutionalized, its practitioners point to the dangers of doing anything about the predicament, lest a reduction in deficits cause a calamity. Students of abnormal psychology will recognize similarity to neurotic behavior, including strong resistance to change.

The 1991 federal budget deficit, including the cost of the savings and loan bailout, has been estimated at $231 billion. Even this figure understates the scope of the problem, for it relies on trust fund surpluses from Social Security, government employees and railroad workers pensions, and veterans life insurance to hide the truth. These trust funds, which have grown rapidly in recent years, belong to participants in those programs, not to the federal government. They are needed to meet future funding requirements. The avoidance of deceptive government accounting practices in relation to the trust funds would bring the real operating budget deficit in 1991 to an estimated $380 billion.

The costs of the 1991 federal deficit may be summarized as follows: (1) Real operating budget deficit, $380 billion; (2) Estimated net loss of U.S. assets to foreigners, $50 billion; (3) Foreign trade deficit, $75 billion; (4) Estimated higher interest expenses to the government and the private sector, $150 billion; (5) Estimated inflation costs, $200 billion. Total estimated costs of $855 billion far exceed the estimated economic growth of two percent, which would add $100 billion to gross national product. Under present circumstances, deficit spending is a disastrous policy which undermines the government's finances, dissipates the nation's wealth on a massive scale, and enriches foreigners at the expense of the American people.

Questions and Answers

1. Isn't deficit spending necessary to keep the economy growing?

Answer: Not at all. As has been shown, the huge budget deficit is the main obstacle to healthy economic growth by the private sector. This deficit is primarily responsible for higher interest rates, inflationary pressures, and foreign trade deficits, all of which harm the private sector. Balancing the federal budget would be the greatest contribution the government could make to strengthening the economy.

2. However harmful budget deficits might be, wouldn't their elimination reduce demand for goods and services from the private sector?

Answer: While the demand from the government would decline, the private sector would generate new sources of economic stimulation. For example, lower defense spending might be replaced by increased demand for fuel-efficient vehicles, particularly if we implemented a substantial gasoline tax increase. Lower interest rates, which would accompany reduced borrowing by the federal government, would stimulate capital spending, housing and construction, and many other enterprises. Moreover, under present circumstances, reduced government spending would lessen our dependence on imported goods and enable U.S. companies to compete more effectively with foreigners at home and abroad. *A balanced budget, particularly one achieved primarily through lower defense spending and higher gasoline taxes, would restore the government's role to one of maximizing the interests of its own people, rather than unwittingly, and witlessly, making foreigners the main beneficiaries of its actions.*

3. In the distant past, when the government operated on a balanced budget basis, didn't we experience cyclical movements in the economy, including recessions?

Answer: Of course we did. In a free enterprise economy, periods of economic growth are followed by recessionary phases. The latter fulfill the function of correcting distortions and excesses that were built up during the upswing. Uninterrupted economic growth is neither attainable nor desirable. The attempt by government to interfere in this process is counterproductive. *Periodic recessions are far preferable to government manipulation of the economy, huge budget deficits, and the dissipation of the nation's wealth.*

Interview with Democrat (DEM)

Dr. O: What do you think of the current budget deficits?

DEM: They are much too high. When we had Democratic presidents, deficits were much lower than they have been in recent years under the Republicans.

Dr. O: How did the Democrats keep deficit spending under control?

DEM: By means of realistic policies toward spending and taxes. We kept spending under control and we raised taxes if it was necessary.

Dr. O: Weren't some of your social programs excessive?

DEM: We don't think so. In view of the enormous social problems faced by our society, we need to spend substantial sums on such programs.

Dr. O: Even at the expense of generating budget deficits?

DEM: As long as the deficits are not excessive, we are not worried.

Dr. O: Budget deficits have harmful effects on the government's finances and on the general economy, which hurt all social classes, including the constituents of the Democratic party.

DEM: Actually, the deficits that were incurred during Democratic administrations were far more benign than most people realize. At those times, the federal government gave strong support to social programs by states and local governments. As a result, their budgets were in good shape. In fact, in many years states had budget surpluses, which largely offset the deficits of the federal government. All of this has changed since Reagan came into power. He drastically reduced help to states and local governments, which has undermined their financial condition. Now all levels of government are in the red.

34

Dr. O: If a Democrat were elected president in 1992, what actions do you think he would take to reduce the budget deficit?

DEM: It would depend on the circumstances. Assuming that we had a reasonably well functioning economy, and no major international crisis, he would propose sharp cuts in defense spending. He would also increase taxes on the rich. He would take forceful actions to eliminate the foreign trade deficit.

Dr. O: What would he do about social programs?

DEM: He would propose increased spending on many social programs, particularly those that have been neglected by the Reagan and Bush Administrations.

Dr. O: How would he handle the savings and loan bailout?

DEM: He would try to find a way to make the rich pay for it. They were the main culprits and the beneficiaries. We don't see why the middle class and the poor should bail out the rich.

Dr. O: But many of those whose deposits are being paid by the federal government are people of moderate means.

DEM: We should honor all those obligations. But the cost to the government should be paid by the wrongdoers and the rich.

Dr. O: As you know, the reported deficits understate the real operating budget deficits by counting trust fund surpluses from Social Security, federal employees and railroad workers pension funds, and veterans life insurance as "federal revenues." This procedure misleads the American people about the true scope of the deficits and jeopardizes the long-term integrity of the programs involved. How do you feel about it?

DEM: We should insulate those programs from the budget deficits.

Dr. O: You mean, the trust fund surpluses should not be included in federal revenues?

DEM: That is correct.

Dr. O: If we followed that procedure, the task of balancing the budget would become much more difficult. These trust fund surpluses are currently generating about $150 billion annually, and they are continuing to grow.

DEM: Let me make something clear. We Democrats favor lower budget deficits, but we are not fanatical on the subject.

Dr. O: You mean, if the budget is moderately unbalanced, you would not be overly concerned.

DEM: In fact, some budget deficit might be a good thing.

Dr. O: Why is that?

DEM: Well, it would stimulate the economy. We know from experience that a balanced budget can cause a recession.

Dr. O: We haven't had a balanced budget since 1969. What experience do we have that proves balanced budgets cause recessions?

DEM: I was talking about prior to 1933.

Dr. O: You mean prior to 1933 we had periodic recessions, just as we did after 1933. There is no convincing evidence that recessions were caused by balanced budgets or prevented by unbalanced ones. In reality, recessions are inherent in the free enterprise system. They are an essential part of the economic process. They fulfill the valuable function of correcting excesses.

DEM: But we have learned since 1933 that we can keep recessions from getting out of hand. Budget deficits are effective tools for counteracting the destructive consequences of recessions.

Dr. O: One could make a strong case that both the economy and the government's finances would be better off if we had no budget deficits, and let recessions run their normal course. If you leave them alone, recessions will do a better job of what needs to be done.

DEM: That may sound good in theory, but it wouldn't be so pleasant in practice. In any case, neither political party would remain inactive for long if unemployment rose sharply, as it would in a recession.

Dr. O: Unemployment insurance was designed to take care of that problem.

DEM: That isn't enough to strengthen the economy.

Dr. O: It might be better is we allowed the economy to do its own strengthening. However well-intentioned politicians might be, their efforts to strengthen the economy tend to be wasteful and largely ineffectual.

DEM: We feel more secure when we control economic events than when we are controlled by them. The Republicans may prefer your ideas, but we don't.

Dr. O: What is best for the economy is best for everyone, Democrats as well as Republicans.

DEM: We haven't done so badly with our approach during the past several decades. If the Republicans hadn't messed things up with their uncontrolled deficits, we could have gotten along fine for a long time.

Dr. O: You mean your approach to interfering in the economy was popular with voters and got you elected much of the time. When the Republicans realized this reality, they changed their views and also embraced deficit spending. Now both political parties engage in this irresponsible practice. I agree with you that the Republicans did a far worse job than the Democrats. In fact, they should never have tried to compete with you in this area. The Republican Party and the nation would have been better off if they had not embraced deficit spending.

DEM: Next time we get a chance, we will show them how to do it right.

Dr. O: There may not be any "next time" to practice deficit spending as a regular policy in the future.

DEM: What do you mean?

Dr. O: The government's financial condition will not permit it, nor will an aroused public opinion fed up with wealth dissipation.

DEM: But what would take its place?

Dr. O: Realistic and responsible behavior in relation to the government's finances.

DEM: But where will that leave the economy?

Dr. O: The economy will do just fine if both political parties make a major effort to balance the budget and stop trying to mastermind economic developments.

Interview with Republican (REP)

Dr. O: What do Republicans think of chronic deficit spending?

REP: We are against it. Historically, Republicans have always opposed deficit spending and the majority of our supporters have continued to hold that view.

Dr. O: But the biggest deficits in history were incurred under Republican presidents in recent years.

REP: The deficits were caused primarily by Democrats, who refused to go along with spending cuts in social programs proposed by the Reagan Administration.

Dr. O: During the Reagan era, the deficits resulted principally from the doubling of defense spending and the unwillingness of the Reagan team to raise taxes to pay for it.

REP: You are taking the side of the Democrats on this issue.

Dr. O: I am trying to be truthful. It is unfair to blame the deficits during the Reagan era on the Democrats. The deficits were engineered by Reagan for his own purposes. He adamantly refused to take any actions that would have reduced the deficits except on his own unworkable terms of eviscerating social programs.

REP: Doc, maybe you were biased against Reagan.

Dr. O: I tried my best to help him. If he had followed my advice, he could have balanced the budget with a combination gasoline tax increase and spending cuts of his choice by reducing waste in the government.

REP: The president is too busy to read letters and books from people he does not know.

Dr. O: He got similar advice from some of his own staff, including Budget Director Stockman, who felt decisive actions were needed to avoid chronically huge budget deficits.

REP: Did Stockman recommend gasoline tax increases?

Dr. O: I don't know what kind of tax increases he had in mind. He spoke generally of the need to raise revenues and to cut spending to bring deficits under control.

REP: History has proven the correctness of Reagan's position. His policies produced the longest period of uninterrupted growth in modern times.

Dr. O: This growth was bought with the biggest wealth dissipation in history. It is not a record to be proud of, particularly for a Republican.

REP: The Democrats benefited politically from deficits for

decades and no one criticized them for it. When a Republican does the same thing, he is blamed for incorrect behavior.

Dr. O: Reagan's deficits were far larger than those produced by the Democrats. In fact, during his eight years in office Reagan generated more deficits than all other presidents put together.

REP: It was a difference in degree, not in kind.

Dr. O: It was indeed a difference in kind. As will be shown in the next chapter, Reagan deliberately engineered the deficits for ulterior purposes. In the process, he did great damage to the nation's vital interests. Moreover, Reagan's policies jeopardized the wealth of the private sector. Ultimately, the constituents of the Republican Party, including the business community and the wealthy, will be the main victims of Reaganomics.

REP: They haven't done so badly thus far.

Dr. O: They will eventually.

REP: In what way?

Dr. O: The federal debt in excess of $3,000 billion will undermine all private wealth. At the least, it will necessitate higher taxes. In addition, it will cause inflationary pressures and higher interest rates, which will harm the economy. It undermines the ability of the Federal Reserve to function properly. It makes us excessively dependent on foreigners. As we will show later on, foreigners were the only real beneficiaries of Reagan's policies.

REP: Reagan did not intend to harm private wealth in any way.

Dr. O: I am sure that is true, but his policies nevertheless produced these results. Whenever policies produce unintentioned results, one should examine one's assumptions, because fundamental misconceptions are involved. Reagan and his team were so blinded by their own ideological dogmas that they failed to realize the great harm they were doing to the country and to their constituents.

REP: But most Republicans and the majority of the American people believe that Reagan was a great president and that his budget policies were good for the nation.

Dr. O: Most people were so preoccupied with the growth of the economy that they ignored the heavy price we were paying for this growth. We dissipated several dollars of wealth for each dollar of growth. Once people become aware of these realities, they will see the Reagan era in a different light.

REP: Are you implying that Reagan's departure from traditional Republican ideas on the budget was a fundamental error?

Dr. O: I have no doubt about it.

REP: As you know, President Bush is trying to reduce the budget deficit. He has departed from Reagan's policies by recommending tax increases as part of the package. What do think of that recommendation?

Dr. O: It is very much to President Bush's credit. I only wish he would get more support from his own party on this issue.

REP: Most Republicans in Congress feel that President Bush made a mistake by agreeing to tax increases, particularly so early in the negotiations. He should have held out to the very last moment before agreeing to such action. That way, the blame would have been on the Democrats, not on the Republicans.

Dr. O: But the Democrats refused to play that game. They insisted that President Bush come out with a statement on taxes before they would cooperate in putting together the deficit reduction package.

REP: The Democrats are better politicians than the Republicans.

Dr. O: I doubt whether there is much difference between Democrats and Republicans when it comes to political savvy. I believe the Democrats have a stronger case.

REP: What do you mean?

Dr. O: The real operating budget deficit in 1991 is estimated at $380 billion. Even if one concentrates on the watered-down deficit of $169 billion which is being used as the basis for negotiations, it is clear that tax increases are essential as part of the deficit reduction package.

REP: I still believe Bush should have forced the Democrats to cut social spending before giving in to their demands for tax increases.

Dr. O: They didn't demand tax increases. They merely took the realistic position that the goal of a balanced budget could not be achieved without tax increases. Any rational person would reach the same conclusion. President Bush showed good sense and acted in the best interest of the nation by endorsing tax increases.

REP: But he may have cost us some seats in the next Congress.

Dr. O: The sooner the Republican Party comes to terms with budget realities, the better. For the past decade, Republicans have violated their own principles, as well as concepts of prudent management, when they embraced the unsound ideas of the Reagan ideologues. Republicans should take the lead in restoring soundness to the government's finances and orthodoxy to their own party's budget philosophy.

REP: But we can't balance the budget by ourselves. The Democrats control the Congress. They must do their share as well.

Dr. O: For reasons of their own, the Democrats would like to rid the nation of Reagan's budget legacy. The prospects seem reasonably good that the two parties can work together on this issue.

REP: I am not as optimistic as you.

Dr. O: If the Republican Party won the election in 1992, including control of the Congress, what policies would they implement to balance the budget?

REP: We would make a major effort to eliminate waste from government, which could save tens of billions of dollars. If the international situation continued to improve, we might make some additional cuts in defense spending, though we wouldn't want to go too far in that direction. We want to remain militarily strong. We might also raise some taxes, though only as a last resort and nothing drastic.

Dr. O: When you talk about "waste in government," I assume you mean primarily social programs.

REP: I mean all programs, including defense.

Dr. O: Do you really think that these proposals would suffice to eliminate the $169 billion deficit, much less the real operating budget deficit of $380 billion?

REP: With a Republican Administration and a Republican Congress, we would create so much confidence in the business community that the economy would boom and generate enough growth in federal revenues to balance the budget.

Dr. O: You sound like a born-again Reaganite. Economic growth is not going to balance a budget that has been structurally distorted by excessive defense spending and an inadequate tax base. We must not rely on wishful thinking for balancing the budget. Moreover, it is likely that some time in the near future we are going to experience a recession, regardless of who sits in the White House or who controls the Congress.

REP: If we have a recession, we have no choice but to increase deficit spending.

Dr. O: Now you sound like a Democrat.

REP: Both political parties agree that in time of recession, the government should engage in deficit spending to stimulate the economy.

Dr. O: That has not been the traditional position of the Republican Party. You have embraced these ideas only in the last twenty years.

REP: But everyone agrees that this approach makes the best sense. It isn't a question of political preference, but of economic necessity.

Dr. O: I happen not to agree with that interpretation.

REP: You mean we should let the recession run its couse without increased government spending?

Dr. O: I would go further than that. I would pursue an active course of deficit reduction, whether we have a recession or not.

REP: But that is preposterous. You can't ignore a recession or make it even worse by cutting government spending and increasing taxes.

Dr. O: These "preposterous" actions may be just the right medicine for our economy. However, we shall leave the detailed discussion of this matter for later.

Chapter 3
History's Biggest Wealth Dissipator

The following table depicts wealth dissipation during the Reagan era.

Wealth Dissipation, 1981-1988*
($ billion)

	Real Operating Budget Deficit	Net Sale of U.S. Assets to Foreigners	Wealth Dissipation
1981	85.8	(28.0)	57.8
1982	134.2	(27.5)	106.7
1983	230.8	35.1	265.9
1984	218.2	80.3	298.5
1985	266.4	97.4	363.8
1986	283.0	121.9	404.9
1987	222.4	141.8	364.2
1988	252.9	137.2	390.1
Total	**1,693.7**	**558.2**	**2,251.9**

*Source: *Statistical Abstract of the United States, 1990*

The Reagan Administration believed they had found a new approach to generating perpetual prosperity. In actuality, their policies have created a fool's paradise. They have given the misleading impression of a sound and prosperous economy, when in actuality the nation's future was being mortgaged and its wealth was being dissipated at an alarming rate. These actions bring to mind the biblical story of Esau, who sold his birthright (wealth) for bread and lentils (immediate gratification).

As has been shown in the previous chapter, deficit spending by the government to stimulate economic activity was first proposed by the British economist John Maynard Keynes in the 1930's to cope with the depression. The Reagan Administration's deficit spending differed significantly from the Keynesian approach in the following respects: (1) Its magnitude was far greater; (2) It persisted unabated after the economy was rolling along at a fast clip; and (3) It was used for ulterior political purposes.

The Reagan Administration incurred more budget deficits than all previous presidencies put together. In the period 1981-1988, the reported deficits totaled $1,338 billion. Even this huge amount understated the truth by $356 billion. The latter represented the trust fund surpluses of such programs as Social Security, federal employees and railroad workers pension funds, and veterans life insurance, which were counted as "federal revenues," even though they did not belong to the federal government. These trust fund surpluses have grown significantly in recent years. They have accounted for any "improvements" in the budget deficits that have been reported since 1987. Real operating deficits, excluding trust fund surpluses, have exceeded $200 billion every year since 1983. In 1988, the real budget deficit was $253 billion, not the $155 billion reported.

This trend is continuing during the Bush Administration. In 1989, the real operating deficit was an estimated $270 billion, about $120 billion more than the reported data. The government has been using trust fund surpluses to disguise the fact that it has failed to take appropriate steps to bring the real budget deficit under control. While deceptive reporting of federal deficits is nothing new, the magnitude of the amounts involved is unprecedented.

President Reagan came into office in 1981, when the U.S. was suffering from a recession that was primarily caused by the oil price escalation of 1979-80 and by the tight monetary policy of the Federal Reserve to cope with the resulting inflationary pressures. The Reagan Administration dealt with this challenge by massive tax cuts and sharply increased defense spending. These measures stimulated the economy and caused an upsurge in budget deficits. If President Reagan had been guided by prudent financial management, he would have taken steps to reduce the deficits once the economy was rolling along. Even Keynesian theory would have supported such action. However, Reagan decided to keep deficits in place.

The Reagan Administration had a hidden agenda for continuing deficits when they were no longer needed for stimulating the economy. The deficits gave President Reagan a large measure of control over the budget process. Professor Milton Friedman, who had close ties to President Reagan, stated candidly, "We believe the (budget) deficit has been the only effective restraint on congressional spending" ("Why the Deficits Are a Blessing," *Wall Street Journal,* December 14, 1988). When Professor Friedman and other supporters of the Reagan Administration wrote about "congressional spending," they were referring to spending on social programs. They ignored the $800 billion increase in defense spending, which was a top priority of the Reagan Administration. The defense spending spree, which brought total espenditures for the military to about $1,900 billion during the Reagan era, was the largest single cause of budget deficits. However, President Reagan did not want to acknowledge that reality publicly. Instead, he blamed the Congress for not cutting social programs sufficiently to make up for the increased defense spending. President Reagan was a master at blaming others for his own budget-busting policies.

The hidden agenda for using deficits to manipulate the Congress was also involved in President Reagan's adamant opposition to tax increases. This orientation was highlighted by the following remarks of Howard H. Baker, Jr., the White House Chief of Staff in the period 1987-1988. Mr. Baker stated, "For my own self-protection, I've never urged him (President Reagan) to raise taxes. But I give him those options. When you get to that part of the presentation (i.e., tax increase proposals), you see visible evidence that his blood pressure rises and you see a very determined president who says 'I'm just not going to do that.'" (*Wall Street Journal,* July 31, 1987).

Reagan's deficit spending policies were facilitated by decades of preoccupation with economic growth and by the fear of recession. This orientation encouraged uncritical acclaim for positive results on current economic activity, even though the costs were much higher than the benefits.

In modern times, the current performance of the economy has been the main focus of attention by politicians, the mass media, and most economic thinkers. As long as economic growth, employment, profits, and other indicators of current economic activity were satifactory, very few individuals would raise questions about the nation's wealth. The Reagan Administration carried this orientation to an extreme. In its endeavor to go all-out for current performance, it eagerly embraced policies that dissipated the nation's wealth. It acted like a business that ignored its balance sheet in the process of going on a spending spree for expansion. Such a business is headed for financial trouble. The same comment is applicable to a government which engages in such irresponsible actions.

The practitioners of the Reagan Administration's policies have ignored the lessons of classical economic thinkers. Adam Smith, the father of the free enterprise theory, opposed policies that caused government deficits and the accumulation of debt. Based on historical evidence, he considered government debt a threat to private wealth and ultimately to the very existence of the state. He would have condemned in the strongest possible terms government policies that deliberately engineered deficits to gain ulterior political objectives.

A financially sound government is an essential precondition to secure private wealth. One cannot construct lasting private prosperity with policies that impoverish the public sector. The Reagan Administration's attempts to strengthen the private sector by weakening the government's finances was irrational and self-destructive behavior. It was a form of warfare against the most vital interests of the American people.

The main beneficiaries of the Reagan Administration's budget policies were those individuals and governments who were not subject to its control, namely foreigners. By following policies antithetical to those of the Reagan Administration, our foreign trading partners and military allies were able to accumulate much of the wealth that was being dissipated by the U.S This topic will be considered in the next chapter.

The Reagan Administration has the dubious distinction of having dissipated more wealth than any other government in history. In just eight years, they added $1.7 trillion to the national debt and caused the net loss of about $560 billion U.S. assets to foreigners.

The main cause of this disastrous performance was the dominance of ideology over realism in relation to the budget. Reagan's policies remind one of the ancient Latin saying "Quo deus vult perdere prius dementat," which translates into "Those whom God wishes to destroy, he first makes mad." If the American people value their remaining wealth, their democratic institutions, and their independence, they had better demand from their representatives in government realistic policies that will restore soundness to the nation's financial affairs.

Questions and Answers

1. Didn't President Reagan inherit the deficits from the Carter Administration?

Answer: No. During its four years in office, the Carter Administration generated $181 billion budget deficits. President Reagan has produced greater budget deficits in *one* year than

President Carter did in *four*.

The deficits that have characterized the Reagan era cannot be blamed on anything other than its own misguided policies. This dismal record was all the more inexcusable in view of the fact that President Reagan professed to run on a balanced budget platform and had a strong mandate from the American people to accomplish this goal.

2. Didn't President Reagan place high priority on balancing the budget?

Answer: President Reagan often spoke about his commitment to a balanced budget, but he was not prepared to take any realistic steps that would have been necessary to accomplish this objective. His talk was a combination of wishful thinking about economic growth supposedly eliminating the deficit and deceptive tirades designed to blame others for his own irresponsible behavior. He was unprepared to work with the Congress on implementing a realistic deficit reduction program that would have included broadly based spending cuts and tax increases.

3. Do you think President Reagan was influenced by Keynesian theory?

Answer: Not at all. I doubt whether Reagan ever read any of the books by Keynes. However, Reagan obviously liked the political gains that resulted from lower taxes and higher government spending on defense, which produced the deficits. A politician does not have to know anything about Keynesian theory to embrace deficit spending for his own purposes. In fact, most politicians, including Reagan, would have rejected the ideas of Keynes, particularly those that advocated higher taxes and budget surpluses during times of strong economic activity.

4. How important was ideology in President Reagan's orientation to the budget?

Answer: Ideology played a major role in President Reagan's approach to budget matters. His ideological orientation made his views dogmatic, simplistic and inflexible. These attributes were not conducive to realistic behavior in dealing with the budget. Government spending and revenues were inherently complex issues. They should be dealt with in a pragmatic, flexible fashion. President Reagan's approach led to confrontations with the Congress. The national interest would have been served much better if he had been more cooperative and compromising.

Most American Presidents had ideological *preferences,* but they have generally avoided ideological *dogmatism,* particularly in relation to the budget. The democratic form of government requires an attitude of give-and-take, of allowing for different points of view to be included in the budget process. Ideological preferences are compatible with this process; ideological dogmatism is not. Ideological dogmatism is an uncompromising orientation, which is characteristic of authoritarianism. President Reagan's approach to the budget departed from democratic traditions. In fact, one could make a possible case for questioning the constitutionality of Reagan's actions in relation to the budget.

5. What does the Constitution say about budget matters?

Answer: Article I, Section 8 of the U.S. Constitution gives the Congress all the specific powers in relation to the budget, including the power "to lay and collect taxes... to pay debts and provide for the common defense and general welfare of the United States." The Constitution does not give the president any specific powers in relation to the budget. This approach to budget issues by the constitutional fathers was quite deliberate. They wanted budget matters to be determined by the Congress, which they felt would most closely reflect the wishes of the people. They did not want the president to have too much power over budget issues. President Reagan's refusal to work with the Congress in dealing with budget deficits, his confrontational tactics, his unwillingness to consider tax increases and broadly based spending cuts, seriously undermined the procedures specified in the Constitution for dealing with the budget process.

6. Haven't most presidents in modern times played a predominant role in the budget process?

Answer: Yes, they have. But no other president was as rigidly ideological as Reagan, nor was anyone as unwilling to work with the Congress on dealing with unprecedented budget deficits.

7. Throughout his years in office, President Reagan was dealing with a Congress dominated by the Democrats. Don't you think that reality had a great deal to do with his tactics?

Answer: It undoubtedly played a role. However, the record shows that Reagan's approach to the budget was not supported by a great many Republicans. On several occasions, Reagan's budget proposals, with their emphasis on slashing social programs, were overwhelmingly defeated by both Houses of Congress, including most Republicans.

8. What is the historic position of the Republican Party in relation to the budget?

Answer: The Republican Party has traditionally made a balanced budget the centerpiece of its agenda. In fact, Republican Adminstrations have generally favored repaying outstanding federal debt. For example, most of the debts incurred during the First World War were paid off during Republican Administrations in the 1920's.

Republican presidents generally tried to control spending on all government programs. They emphasized efficiency, the reduction of waste, and a businesslike approach to management. They did not single out only one category of spending for cuts, while leaving others untouched. If the deficits were so large and so persistent that spending cuts alone did not bring the desired results of balancing the budget, Republican presidents have not hesitated to recommend tax increases.

In many respects, President Reagan's budget policies were contrary to the traditions of the Republican Party. They also violated all principles of sound and prudent management of government affairs.

9. Why did Reagan have so much difficulty with the Congress on budget matters?

Answer: Most of the key players in the Reagan Administration were former businessmen. They apparently had the notion that the President's role in relation to the Congress was analogous to that of a corporation chief to his staff. In private industry, the company's president has the final word on how much money is to be spent for each project or function. This analogy does not hold for the relationship between the President of the U.S. and the Congress. Far from being an inferior branch of government, the Constitution makes the Congress the primary player in relation to the budget. If one wants to draw an analogy, the Congress is more akin to the Board of Directors which determines overall budget policy and allocates financial resources, as well as raising revenues. The president is supposed to execute the laws of the land, as passed by the Congress. If he refuses to cooperate with the Congress, he might well be subject to disciplinary action.

10. President Reagan was elected twice by overwhelming majorities. Doesn't that fact change the rules of the game on budget matters?

Answer: Popular support has no bearing on the constitutionality of budget policies. The Constitution makes it very clear that the Congress has primary control over budget matters and that the President is to execute the laws of the land. If the American people want to change the Constitution, they should follow the procedures for such change as spelled out in the Constitution. Until such constitutional changes are implemented, the Congress, the President, and the American people are obligated to play by the rules spelled out in the Constitution. If we ignore this reality, we may end up with an unconstitutional form of government.

11. Can we learn anything from Reagan's budget policies?

Answer: Reagan went to such extremes on deficit spending that he brought into sharper focus the malaise that had afflicted the nation for a long time. Moreover, his specific policies in relation to budget issues, notably his defense spending spree and his anti-tax fanaticism, were so unsound that they may facilitate the implementation of corrective actions. In effect, by doing the opposite of what Reagan favored, one may be near the correct position.

Reagan's Wrong Assumptions

Unsound assumptions contributed to the massive dissipation of wealth during the Reagan era. In general, these assumptions favored an orientation that placed primary emphasis on current results and ignored harmful long-term consequences. If we want to deal realistically with the budget predicament, we must understand the nature of these wrong assumptions.

1. Growth should be the overriding goal of economic policies.

The Reagan Administration apparently went on the assumption that economic growth would solve all problems. Growth became an obsession. It was the main or sole yardstick by which policies were judged. Any action that stimulated growth was considered desirable and anything that interfered with growth was rejected. Budget deficits were justified because they contributed to a growing GNP. A similar argument was used in support of the sale of U.S. assets to foreigners. Tax increases were rejected because they would interfere with growth.

Harmful consequences: Growth at any price leads to wealth

dissipation, which took place on an unprecedented scale during the Reagan era. It is very dangerous to rationalize wrong policies, like huge budget deficits or the massive sale of assets to foreigners, on the basis of their contribution to growth. Furthermore, this approach is fundamentally flawed in terms of economic realities. It is normal for the economy to go through cycles of expansion and contraction. Any interference with this process by government action is likely to be counterproductive.

2. Increased defense spending can be funded through economic growth.

The Reagan Administration increased defense spending by $150 billion a year. It refused to raise taxes to pay for this program. Instead, it purportedly relied on increased revenues from the growing economy to finance these expenditures.

Harmful consequences: The hoped-for results did not take place. Instead, the nation experienced huge budget deficits. Throughout the Reagan era, no attempt was ever made to correct this fundamental error. Instead, President Reagan used the deficits to put pressure on social spending and to blame the Congress for the deficits. To deal with the legacy of unfunded defense spending, we should give serious consideration to cutting such spending drastically and/or raising sufficient taxes to pay for it.

3. Tax increases should be avoided.

Reagan took an adamant stand against tax increases. He expressed the view that additional taxes would merely encourage more spending on social programs. He also believed that taxes would harm the economy by transferring funds from the private sector to the government. His actions indicated that he gave preference to borrowing and deficits over taxes.

Harmful consequences: Increased government borrowing and huge budget deficits do far more harm to the nation than higher taxes. In fact, taxes should have been increased to pay for the upsurge in defense spending. Reagan refused to acknowledge that reality. His claim that increased taxes would lead to more spending is contradicted by the fact that he had already done the spending on defense. If the defense spending spree had been properly funded with tax increases, the nation would have been spared much of the wealth dissipation that took place in the Reagan era.

4. The sale of U.S. assets to foreigners benefits the economy.

The Reagan Administration welcomed the massive sale of U.S. assets to foreigners. This action helped to stimulate economic growth. It was also considered a positive manifestation of the globalization of financial markets. Last but not least, it provided good prices to sellers and large fees to intermediaries.

Harmful consequences: The $570 billion net U.S. assets sold to foreigners during the Reagan era will generate annual earnings that flow into foreign hands and represent a continuing drain on the U.S. economy. Furthermore, the excessive rate of such asset sales in recent years poses an increasing threat to the financial, economic, and political independence of the U.S. No self-respecting people should allow its assets to be dissipated for the wrongheaded purpose of perpetuating irresponsible budget policies by its government.

5. New theories are better than classical economic doctrines in dealing with budget problems.

Harmful consequences: Classical doctrines have stood the test of time; new theories have not. The admonition against government debt by Adam Smith and other classical thinkers was sound. All attempts by others to justify deficit spending are fundamentally flawed and do great damage to the nation's vital interests. In the past, new theories designed to justify deficit spending and debt accumulation have usually been propounded by those who were critical of the establishment because they had little or no stake in the accumulated wealth. It is rare for conservatives to embrace ideas and policies that jeopardize established wealth. The Reagan Administration has the dubious distinction of having fallen into that trap. Its legacy of unprecedented budget deficits, enormous debt load, and massive wealth dissipation constitute a major threat to all private wealth. The policies that led to this legacy were irresponsible, irrational, and self-destructive. They will ultimately do great harm to the very people who supported Reagan, namely the business community and those with wealth.

Interview with Democrat

DEM: In choosing Reagan as their standard bearer, the Republicans broke a tradition of American politics.

Dr. O: What tradition?
DEM: Previously, both political parties had avoided selecting ideological extremists for the presidency. With Reagan, the Republicans turned their backs on this practice.

Dr. O: What were the effects of this action?
DEM: In addition to the harmful financial and economic consequences you have mentioned, it had negative repercussions on the functioning of the government.

Dr. O: Would you please elaborate?
DEM: The content of Reagan's policies, as well as his tactics, made it very difficult for the two parties to work together in governing the nation. We spent most of our time fighting rather than cooperating. It poisoned the atmosphere and interfered with doing a good job of governing the country.

Dr. O: How did Reagan approach the budget process?
DEM: Reagan's budget proposals contained drastic cuts in social programs, big additions to defense spending, and no tax increases. The Congress spent considerable time trying to find some compromise, but Reagan was adamant in refusing tax

increases and in curbing defense spending. He used confrontational tactics and accused the Congress of busting the budget,
even though he was the one that caused the problem. He
apparently failed to realize that his approach antagonized the
Congress, who resented being pushed around by the President.
Even some of the Republicans were not too happy with the
situation.

Dr. O: Don't you think he knew what he was doing?

DEM: He probably had his own rationale for his actions,
but whatever it was, it did not sit well with the Congress.

Dr. O: What was Reagan trying to accomplish?

DEM: His top priorities were to build up the military, stimulate the economy, and help the rich get richer.

Dr. O: He seemed to have achieved all of those objectives.

DEM: But he mortgaged the nation's future with the biggest
deficits in history.

Dr. O: Haven't the rich always been one of the main
constituencies of the Republican Party?

DEM: Of course, but in the past they didn't go to the extremes
practiced by Reagan and his supporters. Reagan tried his best
to rig government policy in favor of the rich. It seemed as
if he were trying to transform our government from a democracy
to a plutocracy: government of the people, by the rich, and
for the rich.

Dr. O: How far did he get with this approach?

DEM: He went pretty far. The tax laws were restructured
to favor the rich. Restraints on business were weakened or
removed, making possible unfettered greed that enriched the
few at the expense of the general public.

Dr. O: When the Democrats win an election, don't they also

58

reward their constituencies? Isn't it a general rule of politics that to the victor belong the spoils?

DEM: With Reagan, everything was more crass, more extreme.

Dr. O: Do you think Reagan was much harder to deal with than other Republican presidents?

DEM: Definitely. We got along quite well with Ford and with Eisenhower. Even Nixon, whom most Democrats disliked, was someone with whom one could reach reasonable compromises on budget issues. Reagan was the only one who made it virtually impossible to get along and govern the nation in a decent manner. He seemed to relish the fights with the Congress.

Dr. O: How would you rate President Bush in relation to cooperating with the Congress on budget matters?

DEM: Bush is a traditional Republican. I believe Democrats can work with him. However, Reagan's legacy will stand in the way for quite a while.

Dr. O: Can you give an illustration?

DEM: Take the matter of taxes. Any sensible person knows that the budget cannot possibly be balanced without tax increases. Reagan has left the legacy of opposition to all tax increases, a position that has been embraced by the majority of Republicans. They want to blame any tax increases on the Democrats in order to gain political advantages.

Dr. O: Maybe these tactics will backfire. According to the polls, most Americans believe that taxes must be raised to help balance the budget. If the Democrats can depict their opponents as irresponsible anti-tax fanatics who are unqualified to govern, they might actually gain votes.

DEM: That is easier said than done. Taxes are a touchy subject for a politician.

Dr. O: If you assure the voters that the tax increases will be dedicated to deficit reduction and will be combined with spending cuts, you may find considerable support.

DEM: But we can't completely ignore the need for more spending on sadly neglected social programs.

Dr. O: It is a matter of priorities. Under present circumstances, the emphasis should be placed on making the American people aware of the fact that their financial resources, their freedom, and their independence are being threatened by the continuation of present budget policies. Within that framework, they are likely to support tax increases and other necessary measures.

DEM: The Democrats will do their share to restore soundness to the government's finances. We know that everything else depends on a resolution of that problem. I hope we can make quick and decisive progress.

Dr. O: I am confident that if both parties work together, they can find satisfactory solutions to the nation's problems.

Interview with Republican

Dr. O: Do you know how much U.S. wealth is controlled by Republicans?

REP: I have not seen any statistics on that subject.

Dr. O: Would you say it is reasonable to assume that Republicans control more than half of the nation's wealth?

REP: That is a reasonable assumption.

Dr. O: Therefore, Republicans have a major stake in safeguarding that wealth, in protecting it from harm?

REP: That is undoubtedly true.

Dr. O: Because Republicans have had a major stake in wealth

throughout modern American history, they have been looked upon by their constituents and by the American people as a whole as guardians of the nation's wealth.

REP: I would agree that our constituents looked to us to safeguard their wealth, but I am not sure about the American people as a whole.

Dr. O: The Republicans are a minority party. The only way they can win elections is by attracting independents and even some Democrats. One of the main attractions of the Republican Party is that it has traditionally provided assurance that the nation's wealth would be in good hands under their stewardship.

REP: I suppose that is true, particularly in view of the fact that much of the time the Democrats have acted irresponsibly in the financial area.

Dr. O: Deficit spending as a deliberate policy was an invention of the Democrats under the New Deal. Most Republicans, and probably a majority of Americans, have felt uneasy about deficit spending from the very beginning. They saw it as a threat to wealth. Therefore, it is all the more regrettable that Reagan embraced this bad policy and made it infinitely worse by going all-out in that direction.

REP: Why is deficit spending a threat to wealth?

Dr. O: Because the deficits accumulate in the form of federal debt, which is a potential liability of the private sector. In one way or another the private sector has to pay for the public debt, whether in the form of taxes, inflation, or expropriation of property. The greater the public debt, the more dangerous the implications for private wealth. Classical economists like Adam Smith have recognized this reality more than two centuries ago. All Republican presidents up to and including Eisenhower were guided by the philosophy that budget deficits were harmful and should be avoided.

REP: But Nixon recognized that this approach was out-of-date and favored the Democrats politically. He legitimatized deficit spending for Republicans.

Dr. O: Nixon's understanding of economics left something to be desired.

REP: But he was an astute politician. His deficit spending policy helped him win reelection. It served Reagan equally well.

Dr. O: It also opened the floodgates to debt accumulation and placed all private wealth in jeopardy. In the process, it undermined the tradition of the Republican Party as the guardian of the nation's wealth.

REP: We Republicans were merely playing a game the Democrats had invented. We showed them we could do it better than they.

Dr. O: Some games are not worth playing, particularly if they violate important principles and the trust of the nation.

REP: But Republicans were always ready to stop the game if the Democrats agreed to cut back on social spending.

Dr. O: Cutting back on social spending may be a legitimate objective of Republicans, but it should not have priority over balancing the budget. The Reagan Administration made a fundamental mistake in trying to justify huge budget deficits with the rationalization that they were putting pressure on the Democrats to cut social spending. In actuality, Reagan accomplished little in terms of reducing social spending and he saddled the nation with the worst deficits in history. His approach was counterproductive.

REP: Doc, you don't understand how strongly Reagan and his supporters felt about the unfairness of social spending.

Dr. O: What was unfair about social spending?

REP: The Democrats would pass legislation to increase

social spending. Then they would increase taxes to pay for these programs. Most of the taxes would be paid by Republicans. The Democrats would get the credit for the programs, while the Republicans paid the bills. This procedure infuriated Reagan and many other Republicans.

Dr. O: Was there anything new about this tactic?
REP: It has been going on since the beginning of the New Deal.

Dr. O: You mean, the Democrats had engaged in passing social legislation and making Republicans pay for much of it for almost fifty years before Reagan became president?
REP: That is right. But Reagan was the first one to really tackle this issue head-on. He had a strong sense of mission about it. This attitude obviously struck a responsive chord, because Republicans enthusiastically nominated him twice as their presidential candidate.

Dr. O: Why do you think Reagan felt so strongly about this matter?
REP: Because it made good sense. It was about time that Republicans started looking out for their own best interests.

Dr. O: Don't you think Eisenhower also acted in the best interests of the Republican Party?
REP: Of course he did, but he failed to make an issue of fairness in regard to social spending.

Dr. O: What happened to social spending while Eisenhower was in office?
REP: Eisenhower did a pretty good job of keeping such spending under control.

Dr. O: Did Eisenhower do as good a job as Reagan in this matter?

REP: Eisenhower probably accomplished more than Reagan in keeping social spending under control. But he operated in a low-keyed fashion. Reagan brought the issue into the limelight, and Republicans got a big charge out of it.

Dr. O: If I understand you correctly, you are saying that Eisenhower may have accomplished more than Reagan in keeping social spending under control, but his low-keyed approach was not as satisfying to Republicans as Reagan's high profile attacks on social spending.
REP: That is correct.

Dr. O: In other words, Republicans were more eager to get emotional gratification than in reducing social spending or balancing the budget.
REP: Emotional gratification is important in politics. It leads to greater enthusiasm and increased financial suport. One shouldn't underestimate its significance.

Dr. O: I don't. In fact, it may help to clarify why Republicans, who are usually conservative and realistic on financial matters, were seduced into supporting policies that loaded the government down with huge debts and jeopardized all private wealth.
REP: Do you mean that their emotional response to Reagan blinded them to financial realities?

Dr. O: That may well have been the case.
REP: But don't you think it was about time that somebody stood up to the Democrats and put a halt to their wasteful social spending?

Dr. O: That goal could have been accomplished much more effectively with a different approach.
REP: How do you mean?

Dr. O: Let's assume that Bush had been elected president in 1980.

REP: What would he have done about social spending in particular, and the budget in general?

Dr. O: Bush would probably have arranged a series of meetings with Congressional leaders of both political parties and presented them with the following scenario: (1) We all agree that we need to increase defense spending (leaders of both political parties shared that view in the early 1980's.) (2) We inherited a budget deficit of $58 billion from the Carter era. We want to see what we can do to reduce that amount (both parties felt that $58 billion of annual red ink was too much). (3) We have only two alternatives to accomplish these objectives: (a) Raise taxes and/or (b) Cut spending on social programs. Let's see what we can work out together.

REP: Do you think the Democrats would have gone along with that approach?

Dr. O: I am confident they would have responded favorably. The net result would have been a strong defense program, some reduction in social spending, some tax increases, and low budget deficits.

REP: But the tax increases would have been largely at the expense of our constituents.

Dr. O: Not necessarily. Bush and the Congress might have agreed to lower income tax rates, while eliminating most deductions, as was done in 1986. Consumption taxes, particularly on gasoline and on luxuries, might have provided the additional revenues needed to balance the budget.

REP: I don't recall Bush ever having advocated increased taxes on gasoline or on luxuries.

Dr. O: As part of an overall package, he might have accepted such taxes. We are assuming that Bush would have given top priority to balancing the budget, which would be in line with his basic orientation.

REP: But Bush stated emphatically during the 1988 campaign that he would not raise taxes.

Dr. O: He made no such statements when he ran against Reagan in the Republican primaries of 1980. In fact, he called Reagan's approach to the budget "voodoo economics."

REP: Bush and his team are good at coining phrases that he subsequently regrets having made.

Dr. O: An objective appraisal of Reagan's budget policies would indiate that Bush's term "voodoo economics" was quite appropriate. But getting back to our hypothetical arrangement between Bush and the Congress in 1981, we could have avoided most of the wealth dissipation that has plagued this nation during the past decade.

REP: These are interesting speculations about what could have been in the past. But we can't turn the clock back. Where do we go from here?

Dr. O: Republicans have another opportunity to work with Bush. He is now trying to work out an arrangement with the Democrats to balance the budget over the next few years.

REP: But the Democrats are not cooperating very well. In fact, thus far they have let Bush make all the concessions, while they have yet to show their hand.

Dr. O: But the majority of Republican members of Congress have already told President Bush that they would not support tax increases. They are still caught up in the confrontational tactics of the Reagan era.

REP: If you want to beat the Democrats, you have to be tougher and shrewder than they.

Dr. O: Not necessarily. The Democrats were browbeaten

by Reagan for eight years and they are very suspicious of some key players on the Bush team. Bush knows the Democrats very well; after all, he was in the Congress with them for many years. A kind and gentle approach may be just right. I think the Republicans should have more faith in their President and support him in his efforts to work with the Congress on balancing the budget.

REP: Do you think they will come to an agreement?

Dr. O: Probably.

REP: Will it solve the budget problem?

Dr. O: It will be a step in the right direction, but it will fall far short of being a real solution. If we want to stop dissipating our wealth, we will have to do much more. We will discuss this matter in subsequent chapters.

Chapter 4
Wealth Dissipation Benefits
Foreigners at U.S. Expense

Foreigners have been the main beneficiaries of the wealth dissipation policies of the U.S. In the 1970's foreign oil producers got the lion's share of squandered U.S. wealth. In the 1980's, our military allies and trading partners in industrial countries were enriched by U.S. wealth dissipation. This chapter will focus on adverse developments during the Reagan era, 1981-1988.

As the following table shows, the U.S. merchandise trade deficit in the period 1981-1988 totaled almost $800 billion. Like the budget deficits, this amount was unprecedented and exceeded by far all previous trade deficits put together. As will be shown, the budget policies of the Reagan Administration were primarily responsible for the trade deficits.

U.S. Merchandise Trade Deficits, 1981-1988*
($ billion)

1981	28.0
1982	36.4
1983	67.1
1984	112.5
1985	122.1
1986	145.1
1987	159.5
1988	127.2
Total	**797.9**

*The data in this table, as well as the two that follow, were taken from *The Statistical Abstract of the United States, 1990*

These U.S. trade deficits represented surpluses to foreigners, who were able to use these funds to make increased investments in the U.S. In the process, the U.S. was transformed from the world's leading creditor to its biggest debtor. These data are revealed in the next table.

International Asset Transactions, 1981-1988
($ billion)

	Foreign Assets Acquired by U.S.	U.S. Assets Acquired by Foreigners	Balance
1981	111.0	83.0	28.0
1982	121.2	93.7	27.5
1983	49.8	84.9	(35.1)
1984	22.3	102.6	(80.3)
1985	32.6	130.0	(97.4)
1986	99.7	221.6	(121.9)
1987	76.2	218.0	(141.8)
1988	82.1	219.3	(137.2)
Total	**594.9**	**1,153.1**	**(558.2)**

Foreign assets acquired by the U.S. declined sharply in the period 1983-1985 and recovered somewhat thereafter. In contrast, foreign acquisition of U.S. assets showed dramatic increaes, reaching a level in excess of $200 billion in the last three years of the period covered. The balance of asset transactions has favored foreigners since 1983.

A similar trend can be observed in income flows from foreign assets, as shown in the following table.

Income Flows from International Investments, 1981-1988
($ billion)

	To U.S.	To Foreigners
1981	86.4	52.3
1982	83.5	54.9
1983	77.3	52.4
1984	85.9	67.4
1985	88.8	62.9
1986	88.6	67.0
1987	104.7	82.4
1988	107.8	105.5

Between 1981 and 1988, U.S. income from foreign investments grew from $86 to $108 billion. In the same interval, foreigners doubled their income from U.S. investments, reaching almost par with their U.S. counterparts. They gained in eight years what it took the U.S. most of the 20th century to accomplish.

To place the data from the preceding three tables in perspective, in most of the twentieth century the U.S. enjoyed a favorable balance of trade. Similarly, in the same interval the U.S. was a leading creditor to the rest of the world. Income from foreign investments was a major factor in the favorable U.S. trade balance. All of these variables were drastically altered in an unfavorable direction by the wealth dissipating policies of the Reagan Administration.

The following interrelated factors were involved in this loss of U.S. wealth to foreigners:

1. Disproportionate U.S. spending on defense.
2. Our low gasoline tax.
3. Huge federal budget deficits.
4. Heavy dependence on foreigners to help finance the deficits.
5. High interest rates, which weakened the U.S. competitive position in the international marketplace.
6. Enormous foreign trade deficits, which put vast financial resources into the hands of foreigners.
7. Low value of the U.S. currency, resulting from the foreign trade deficits and from dependence on foreigners for helping to finance budget deficits.
8. Weak U.S. currency enabled foreigners to acquire our assets at bargain prices.

The U.S. spends more on defense than all of its allies put together. In terms of gross national product (GNP), the U.S. has devoted about twice as much to defense as West European countries and six times as much as Japan. A substantial share of U.S. defense spending was applied, directly and indirectly, to the defense of Western Europe and Japan. High U.S. defense spending enabled the Europeans and the Japanese to keep their own expenditures relatively low. In effect, the U.S. was subsidizing its allies on a vast scale. This policy was initiated during the Second World War and has been in effect for almost fifty years. It is noteworthy that the more we spend on defense relative to the expenditures by our allies, the more harmful the results to our wealth. The defense buildup by the Reagan Administration during the 1980's was the largest cause of the wealth dissipating process that has plagued this nation. If we want to reverse this dangerous trend, we must cut back on defense spending, while our allies carry a bigger share of the responsibility for defending themselves. If our allies want us to maintain armed forces on or near their territories, they should pay us for the costs involved. We should no longer provide this expensive service free of charge or on a heavily subsidized basis.

To help place defense spending policies into perspective, if the U.S. were to cut its spending to the West European level in relation to GNP, it would reduce its budget deficit by $150 billion annually. If it followed the Japanese model, the yearly saving would be $250 billion. It is evident from these data that a realistic approach to defense spending is an indispensable prerequisite to sound budget policies and to effective measures for stopping the dissipation of wealth.

Similar comments are applicable to gasoline tax policies. Such taxes average thirty cents per gallon in the U.S., of which the federal government collects nine cents. In contrast, gasoline taxes average about $2 per gallon in Western Europe and Japan. If the U.S. were to raise its gasoline tax to the level prevailing among its major trading partners, it would reduce its budget deficits and associated wealth dissipation by $170 billion annually. If we want to safguard our remaining wealth and our independence, we had better implement a significant increase in our gasoline tax.

Our excessive defense spending and our low gasoline taxes are primarily responsible for the huge real operating budget deficits of the federal government, which are currently (1990) running at an annual rate of about $350 billion. As a result, the government has to borrow about $1 billion a day to meet its financial obligations. The private sectors of the U.S. economy have not generated sufficient savings to take care of their own requirements as well as the needs of the federal government. We have become heavily dependent on foreign funds to help finance the budget deficits.

To attract foreign investors, interest rates have to be kept high enough to compete with alternative options. In 1990, there has been upward pressure on worldwide interest rates because of strong demand for funds from various sources, including the newly emerging market economies of Eastern Europe. Interest rates adjusted for inflation in the main creditor nations,

Japan and West Germany, are already at levels comparable to those prevailing in the U.S. Our status as the world's leading debtor nation restricts the ability of the Federal Reserve to lower interest rates to stimulate the U.S. economy. The responsible way to deal with this predicament is to reduce the U.S. budget deficit, which would lessen our need for borrowing from foreigners.

High interest rates add to the capital and operating costs of business, particularly those enterprises involved in capital-intensive activities, which play a major role in exports. U.S. foreign trade deficits were largely caused by our relatively high interest rates, which were primarily due to our huge budget deficits and the heavy reliance on foreigners to finance them.

The enormous foreign trade deficits and the heavy reliance on borrowing form foreigners to help finance the budget deficits, weakened the value of the U.S. dollar. As a result, foreigners were able to acquire U.S. assets at bargain prices. It is noteworthy that the weakness of the U.S. currency was caused by irresponsible government policies in relation to the budget, not by normal economic trends. This problem can only be solved by correcting government budget policies.

Most people, including the majority of politicians and policy makers, have failed to understand the true nature of the budget predicament confronting the U.S. Therefore, they tend to recommend policies that fail to solve the problem or that make it even worse.

In the past, the government has relied on the Federal Reserve to stimulate the economy during periods of reduced economic activity. While the U.S. had the world's strongest economy and was the world's leading creditor, this approach worked reasonably well. However, we no longer enjoy this status. During the past decade, the U.S. has been transformed into the world's largest debtor. The most dynamic economies in the world today are in Western Europe and Japan, not in the U.S. Under these circumstances, the Federal Reserve can no longer stimulate the U.S. economy at will. It must carefully consider the impact of its policies on our foreign creditors. If the Federal Reserve decides to stimulate the U.S. economy by increasing money and credit and lowering interest rates, foreign investors in U.S. securities (and their U.S. counterparts) may respond by selling their holdings, which would raise interest rates and reduce the funds available for stimulating the economy. The Federal Reserve has become hostage to the foreign creditors of the U.S. Most Americans, including the politicians and policy makers who caused the predicament, have not as yet adjusted to this reality.

The foreign trade deficit has drawn much attention from government officials. The main focus has been on implementing policies designed to force foreigners to open their markets to U.S. goods and services. This approach has been particularly directed at Japan, which has enjoyed huge trade surpluses with the U.S. While the Japanese government has complied with U.S. requests for more open markets, the trade surplus remains very high. This condition is likely to persist as long as the U.S. subsidizes Japan with a defense umbrella equivalent to $120 billion a year. We would be well advised to focus our attention more on that issue and less on nitpicking Japanese economic and cultural practices.

One of the most dangerous traps that many policy makers and economists have fallen into is to rely on a lower dollar to reduce the foreign trade deficit. At first sight, this approach seems logical, for a weak dollar will supposedly stimulate exports and reduce imports. However, in reality the situation is not that simple. A lower dollar tends to raise inflationary pressures, which causes higher interest rates, which increases the costs of U.S. exporters, which makes it more difficult for them to compete in the international marketplace. There are also problems with reducing imports through a lower dollar. Experience has shown that once people are accustomed to foreign goods, they tend to continue purchasing them, even if the price rises. This response is particularly likely if the foreign product enjoys advantages, such as better quality, over their U.S. counterparts. Moreover, foreign producers will make every effort to hold on to their U.S. markets, even if it means lowering their profits to meet the challenge of the weaker dollar.

Last but not least, a weak dollar enables foreigners to acquire U.S. assets at bargain prices. Those who advocate a weak dollar generally tend to ignore this reality or to rationalize it away by claiming that foreign investment is a good thing because it stimulates the U.S. economy. It is indeed true that in the past decade the U.S. has relied heavily on the sale of its assets to foreigners to keep the economy growing. But is economic growth worth the price we are paying? Do we really want to transform our nation into a quasi-colonial entity, with foreigners playing an increasingly important role in our financial, economic, and political affairs, for the purpose of artificially stimulating the economy?

If the American people value their remaining wealth, their freedom, and their independence, they had better demand an end to the irrational budget policies which enrich foreigners at their expense. Common sense and a healthy dose of patriotism, along with the willingness to make some sacrifices, will go a long way to ridding the nation of the irresponsible budget policies that have plagued us during the past decade.

Questions and Answers

1. Were U.S. government officials aware of the fact that budget deficits have enriched foreigners at the expense of the American people?
Answer: U.S. government officials have failed to understand the relationships among budget deficits, foreign trade deficits, the weak dollar, and the loss of assets to foreigners. For example, the harmful impact on U.S. wealth of the Reagan Administration's defense spending spree has not been properly understood to this day. Similarly, policy makers are either unaware of, or ignore, the negative consequences flowing from our low gasoline tax policy, which also undermines our wealth and

enriches our foreign trading partners.

2. How do you explain the fact that our government has failed to understand these dangers?

Answer: Aristotle pointed out 2,500 years ago that if one wants to find the right solution to a problem, one must first ask the right question. U.S. government officials have generally failed to meet this basic test of sound thinking and problem solving. Officials dealing with budget matters rarely consider the international ramifications of their policies. Instead, their main or sole focus of attention is placed on how to achieve a given objective and how to overcome any domestic political obstacles. Moreover, in playing their political games, budget makers are often so preoccupied with their ideological pre-conceptions and/or constituency considerations that they fail to consider the effects on the nation as a whole or the impact on our standing in the international sphere.

For example, the Reagan Administration apparently utilized large budget deficits as a tool with which to exert pressure on Congress to reduce social spending. This orientation per-petuated the budget deficits, which enriched foreigners at U.S. expense. Ideological dogmatism resulted in self-destructive policies which gave foreigners the opportunity to gain advantages over Americans, rich and poor.

Liberal Democrats have their own shortcomings on budget matters. For example, many of them oppose a gasoline tax because of its regressive nature. While it is true that such a tax has a negative impact on the poor who drive cars, it would be very much in the national interest to implement such a tax to help solve the budget deficit, to strengthen energy security, and to improve the environment. The regressive problem can be solved through appropriate measures, such as helping the poor acquire fuel-efficient vehicles. However, some liberal politicians would rather gain the satisfaction of demonstrating ideological purity than dealing realistically with a tax that can bring great benefits to the nation, including the poor.

77

It is noteworthy that the gasoline tax is also opposed by the right wing ideologues, who don't want any tax increase that might reduce budget deficits, lest the pressure is reduced to keep social spending under control. Foreigners are the main beneficiaries of these ideologically motivated approaches to key budget issues.

3. Haven't politicians always been inclined to promote themselves and special interests rather than serving the best interests of the nation?
Answer: It is probably true that most politicians have lacked the qualities of statesmanship that place the national interest ahead of all other considerations. However, I believe the Reagan Administration has added a new dimension to unsound thinking about budget matters by giving top priority to ideological considerations. Spending on social programs was depicted as largely wasteful and harmful to society. In contrast, defense spending was associated with high ideals of patriotism. All taxes were considered to be inherently evil, because they took money from the private sector and gave it to grasping politicians who would procede to spend it on unneeded social programs.

These misleading and largely fallacious ideological notions interfered with realistic actions in relation to budget issues. Their practical significance should not be underestimated. When President Bush recently (June 1990) came out in favor of tax increases as part of a budget balancing package, the majority of Republicans in the Congress were opposed to this action on ideological grounds. These ideological obstacles to pragmatic behavior victimize Americans and enrich foreigners, whose governments are more realistic in dealing with taxes, defense spending, and other budget matters.

4. Are you saying that the dissipation of U.S. wealth and the enrichment of foreigners was solely the fault of our own politicians and policy makers?
Answer: That is essentially correct. Foreigners did not ask the

Reagan Administration to double defense spending. On the contrary, they made it clear that they felt such increases were not necessary. They refused to go on a defense spending spree of their own. Similarly, foreigners did not ask us to keep our gasoline tax so low that their nationals would gain a competitive advantage in the international marketplace. In fact, several foreign governments, including that of Japan, have repeatedly suggested that the U.S. should increase its gasoline tax to help reduce its budget deficit and to lessen wasteful consumption of gasoline. U.S. policies in relation to these issues have been irresponsible and have led to self-destructive consequences.

5. Polls indicate that most Americans are alarmed at the massive transfer of U.S. assets to foreigners. Do you share this concern?
Answer: I do. It seems to me unconscionable that the U.S. should dissipate its assets on the basis of such wrongheaded policies as the deliberate use of deficits to exert pressure against social spending, or the continuation of low gasoline tax levies at a time we are heavily dependent on oil imports. Balancing the federal budget is the only realistic way for putting an end to this wealth dissipation. The American people should demand that their government take appropriate actions along those lines.

6. What do you think of the argument that the transfer of U.S. assets to foreigners is part of the trend toward the globalization of financial and economic markets?
Answer: Since 1981, the flow of assets has been largely a one-way street, from the U.S. to the rest of the world. It looks to me as if the so-called globalization of markets involves a high degree of risk to U.S. independence. We had better be careful, lest globalization results in a form of financial and economic colonization of the U.S. by its trading partners and military allies. To avoid this problem, we should put our financial house in order as soon as possible. Balancing the federal budget should be given top priority.

Interview with Democrat

Dr. O: What do you think of the thesis that foreigners were the main beneficiaries of our irresponsible budget policies during the past decade?

DEM: I believe there is a lot of truth to that statement. However, one should not overlook the fact that big business and the rich in this country have also gained many advantages from these policies.

Dr. O: You mean, U.S. budget policies during the past decade have favored big business and the rich, foreign and domestic, at the expense of the American middle class and poor.

DEM: That is right. They have reversed the Robin Hood philosophy: they take from the poor and give to the rich. Reagan would rather help a rich foreigner than lift a hand for a poor American.

Dr. O: My studies indicate that U.S. business and the rich in this country will ultimately be among the victims of the huge budget deficits, which jeopardize all private wealth.

DEM: In the long run, you may be right, but in the meantime, they have made some tidy profits for themselves, and shared very little of it with the government, thanks to low tax rates on personal income and profits.

Dr. O: Don't you think the Reagan Administration would favor rich Americans over rich foreigners?

DEM: I doubt whether Reagan made any distinction between rich Americans and rich foreigners. He liked all rich people. His policies were designed to make the world safe for the rich. If he had his way, he would have set up a plutocracy, a government of the people, by the rich and for the rich.

Dr. O: Your comments about Reagan are extreme. Perhaps you are letting your imagination run away from reality.

DEM: When it comes to Reagan, one can hardly be suspicious enough. He left a terrible legacy, which will haunt us for years to come. Our problems with foreigners are a major aspect of our predicament.

Dr. O: If the Democrats won the next presidential election, how would they handle the foreign trade deficit?

DEM: We would make sure that foreign trade were carried on in a fair and equitable manner. We would not tolerate chronically high trade deficits with any country. We would insist that they remove all barriers to our goods and services, or we will take countermeasures. We would strictly enforce our trade laws.

Dr. O: My studies indicate that the foreign trade deficits are closely linked to our budget deficits. Our high defense spending subsidizes our affluent allies and has an adverse impact on our foreign trade balance.

DEM: The Democrats favor major cuts in defense spending, particularly in relation to foreign bases. We would take a close look at all aspects of our defense policies. We would be inclined to reduce or eliminate all subsidies to affluent allies.

Dr. O: How do you feel about the massive foreign investment in the U.S.?

DEM: Democrats are concerned about the lopsided nature of this trend during the Reagan and Bush eras. We have nothing against foreign investments provided our laws are obeyed and our businessmen can invest on equal terms in foreign countries. Any nation that keeps our people out while they gobble up our assets will be confronted with the reality that they must reciprocate. We would not tolerate unfair behavior.

Dr. O: How would you compare your policies with those of the Republicans under Reagan and Bush?

DEM: We would place primary emphasis on looking out

for the best interests of the U.S.

Dr. O: You mean, you would pursue a more nationalistic policy than the Republicans?

DEM: You might put it that way. Our first responsibility is to 250 million Americans, whether they are rich, middle class or poor. The Republicans appear to have ignored a lot of our people, particularly the middle class and the poor.

Dr. O: If you had to choose between supporting a rich American and a rich foreigner, to whom would you lend a helping hand?

DEM: The rich American.

Dr. O: You would consider his nationality more important than the fact that he was rich?

DEM: That is right. We don't let our political differences with the rich blind us to the reality that they are Americans and worthy of our respect and support.

Dr. O: Most of our problems with foreign nations, including the large foreign trade deficits and the loss of U.S. assets, can be solved if we took realistic steps to balance the federal budget.

DEM: The Democrats have every intention to move in that direction. We may not go as far as you propose, but we intend to bring the deficits down significantly from current levels. We agree that such action would be the best procedure for reducing our problems with foreigners.

Interview with Republican

Dr. O: What do you think of the thesis that foreigners have been the main beneficiaries of U.S. budget policies since 1981?

REP: The American people have also benefited. We have enjoyed almost eight years of economic growth. Foreign investments in the U.S. have helped to achieve this accomplishment.

Dr. O: But these foreign investments have also given foreigners a major stake in U.S. industry, real estate, and other assets. Economic growth that is based on the sale of assets to foreigners involves serious disadvantages, including curtailment of U.S. independence. The Reagan Administration was too preoccupied with growth, and paid too little attention to adverse consequences.

REP: We are not worried about who owns U.S. assets, as long as the owners abide by our laws and play a constructive role in our economy.

Dr. O: But there is a fundamental difference between ownership of assets by foreigners or by U.S. enterprises.

REP: What is the difference?

Dr. O: The earnings generated by foreign owned assets flow to foreign countries, while those produced by U.S. enterprises stay here. As was shown at the beginning of this chapter, foreign earnings on U.S. assets have shown dramatic growth in recent years.

REP: But the U.S. also gains from economic growth.

Dr. O: Much of the growth in the Reagan era was in the form of defense spending, which has no long-term economic utility. It was a very bad bargain for the U.S., particularly if one considers that much of that spending was incurred to help defend the very foreigners who have acquired our assets.

REP: Defense spending provides us with security against foreign adversaries.

Dr. O: A self-respecting nation should pay for its own defense spending and should limit the amount it devotes to subsidizing foreign nations. We have failed to act realistically in this matter.

REP: The foreigners who invest in the U.S. are our trading partners and our military allies. We consider them to be our friends, like members of our family.

Dr. O: One of the risks concerns the possibility that they may not always be our friends and allies. What would happen if one or more of these nations became adversaries in the future? Their ownership of U.S. assets could prove to be very troublesome.

REP: It would be more of a problem for them than for us. If they became hostile to us, we would confiscate their assets.

Dr. O: You mean, foreign owned assets in the U.S. may be considered inducements for good behavior by foreign nations?

REP: I should think so.

Dr. O: But foreign nationals and governments have their own priorities, which may not necessarily coincide with the best interests of the U.S. For example, let's assume we get into a recession. Foreigners may conclude that the U.S. is not a good place to invest under those conditions. They may decide to stop making new investments or even withdraw existing ones from the U.S. As a result, the U.S. economy might be pushed deeper into the recession.

REP: If that happened, we would consult with our foreign friends to make clear our displeasure with their actions and to ask them to avoid harming our economy.

Dr. O: But they might point out that their nationals are guided by economic considerations that induce them to act in their own best self-interest. They may feel safer investing in their own countries.

REP: I can assure you we would not allow actions that would damage our vital interests.

Dr. O: What could we do?

REP: If need be, we could stop them from withdrawing funds from the U.S.

Dr. O: Such action would undermine our relations with foreigners and would brand us an unreliable place to invest. It would have very harmful consequences for the U.S. economy and for the rest of the world.

REP: We were only talking about a hypothetical situation. I don't think anything like this will happen.

Dr. O: It may be more likely than you think. In any case, it seems to me that too little thought has been given to future contingencies in our rush to sell off U.S. assets as a substitute for realistic actions on the budget.

REP: As you know, the U.S. owns substantial assets in foreign countries. In fact, if one used current values or replacement costs as criteria, our foreign holdings would exceed those of foreigners in the U.S.

Dr. O: U.S. enterprises acquired those foreign holdings over the past hundred years as a natural outgrowth of economic developments. In contrast, the massive loss of U.S. assets to foreigners occurred during the past decade, primarily because of irresponsible budget policies. The American people should demand appropriate actions to balance the budget and to put an end to the reckless behavior in relation to the nation's assets.

REP: Do you mean we should restrict or even prohibit the sale of U.S. assets to foreigners?

Dr. O: If we balance the budget, we won't need to take any such actions.

REP: What if we don't balance the budget?

Dr. O: If we continue to generate huge budget deficits, we will get into an increasingly difficult predicament. As a result, foreigners may lose confidence in the U.S. and reduce their investments here. Such action would deal a serious blow to our economic game plan, which relies on foreign investments for stimulating the economy. We would probably get into an economic slump plus bigger budget deficits.

REP: But foreigners have an important stake in our economy. They wouldn't want to do anything that would jeopardize their own interests.

Dr. O: Foreigners could not bail us out of our predicament, even if they were so inclined. It is up to the American people and their government to straighten out the federal budget. That is the only realistic procedure for coping with our problems, including the loss of assets to foreigners.

REP: We have made significant progress in relation to the foreign trade deficit, which is a major factor in the acquisition of U.S. assets by foreigners. The foreign trade deficit has declined from about $160 billion in 1987 to less than $100 billion currently.

Dr. O: That reduction has been achieved primarily by lowering the value of the dollar. However, this approach is counterproductive, because it makes it easier for foreigners to acquire our assets at bargain prices in terms of their own currencies.

REP: The low value of the dollar may be a necessary price to pay for achieving our goal of balanced foreign trade.

Dr. O: It is necessary only if you continue the asinine budget policies currently prevailing. If we balanced the budget, we could achieve balanced foreign trade with a strong dollar. As a result, we wouldn't need to sell our assets to foreigners at bargain prices.

REP: You keep on harping about the balanced budget as if that were the sole solution to our problems.

Dr. O: That is the truth. Look, the Reagan Administration acted on fundamentally unsound assumptions in relation to the budget. This reality is responsible for all of the problems confronting us, including budget deficits, foreign trade deficits, loss of assets to foreigners, and weakness in the dollar. By taking appropriate actions to balance the budget, we would solve all of these problems. There is no other realistic solution.

PART II. THE SOLUTION:
BALANCING THE BUDGET AND WEALTH ACCUMULATION

The wealth dissipation predicament that has plagued this nation at an unprecedented rate during the past decade was primarily caused by excessive defense spending and by grossly inadequate gasoline taxes. Therefore, it would seem logical to give priority to these issues for helping to find solutions. In Chapter 5 we propose major cuts in defense spending. In Chapter 6 we recommend a substantial increase in the gasoline tax. These proposals are combined with other spending cuts and tax increases to achieve the goal of transforming the nation from wealth dissipation to wealth accumulation. Chapter 7 presents this solution in the form of Option 3, which also contains an innovative approach to solving the savings and loan problem.

Chapter 5
Let's Cut Defense Spending by
$100 Billion a Year

Excessive defense spending is a major cause of the wealth dissipation afflicting the U.S. Reducing such spending by $100 billion annually would greatly improve the budget and the foreign trade balance. Fortunately, such action is facilitated by better relations with the Soviet Union.

The U.S. spends about $300 billion annually on defense, or six percent of the gross national product (GNP). West European nations allied with the U.S. devote about three percent of their GNP to defense, while Japan allocates only one percent of its GNP to this task.

The disproportionate defense spending by the U.S. has historical roots. At the end of the Second World War, the U.S. was the only major power in the Free World which had the resources to safeguard Western Europe and Japan from possible Soviet agression. Ever since, the U.S. has played a predominant role in the military area. In the meantime, our allies have rebuilt their economies. In many instances, their financial situation is better than that of the U.S. Nevertheless, the U.S. has continued to subsidize them with its defense umbrella. This policy is obsolete and harmful to our vital interests.

The undesirable nature of U.S. defense policies is particularly evident in relation to Japan. The U.S. has protected Japan from foreign adversaries as if it were our fifty-first state. However, while the average American contributes about $1,200 annually to pay for the U.S. defense effort, the average Japanese is taxed only $200 a year for defense by his government. The $1,000 difference, which translates into more than $120 billion annually for Japan as a whole, has a great deal to do with that country's economic performance, wealth accumulation, and acquisition of U.S. assets. In effect, for the "privilege" of defending their homeland, the U.S. has enriched the Japanese while impoverishing its own people.

Defense spending is hazardous to a nations wealth and economic well-being. Weapons are very costly to build and generate a stream of expenses throughout their period of use. For example, a warship may cost $100 million to construct and may involve annual expenditures of $10 million for personnel, maintenance, and other operating expenses. Assuming a life of twenty years for this ship, its total cost to the nation will be $300 million. The nation's financial resources are reduced by that amount.

In contrast, any successful commercial investment will add to the nation's wealth. For example, a factory or an office building may cost $100 million to construct. Let us assume that after all expenses, it will generate $10 million profits annually. Over a twenty year period, this enterprise will have generated income totalling $200 million, or $100 million more than the original cost. This sum enriches the proprietors and the nation.

This economic analysis helps to explain the historical fact that all empires based on military might have collapsed and have left their perpetrators impoverished. The wealth-destroying propensity of military spending is so great that even nations that used their might to exploit others have not fared well. The dire economic condition of the empire built by the Soviet Union is the most recent example of the impoverishment which follows in the wake of excessive defense spending.

The U.S. government has undermined its finances and

exploited its own people to continue playing a role in relation to Free World defense that is no longer appropriate. As a result, our allies in Western Europe and Japan have accumulated massive quantities of U.S. assets generating billions of dollars in annual revenues. What does the U.S. have to show for this transfer of wealth to foreigners? We have the dubious distinction of possessing the world's most powerful arsenals of nuclear weapons, missiles, bombers, warships, and tanks. Our most fervent hope for these arsenals is that they may never have to be used, and that we can write the following epitaph on their storage sites: "May they rust in peace."

In recent times, the internationl situation has changed dramatically for the better. The nations of Eastern Europe have gained a substantial degree of freedom and are turning to democratic forms of government and market-oriented economic institutions. The Soviet Union itself is undergoing a profound transformation that holds promise for its own people and for the rest of mankind.

Under these circumstances, U.S. self-interest and that of the Soviet Union have a common denominator: both can benefit greatly from drastic reductions in defense spending. If we cut such spending by $100 billion annually, we would still have sufficient deterrent power to take care of any realistically fore-seeable conditions.

Defense spending played a key role in the wealth dissipation policies of the Reagan Administration and the deceptions accompanying them. President Reagan went all-out for defense, increasing spending for this purpose by $800 billion to a total of $1,900 billion during his term in office. He adamantly refused to raise taxes to pay for this defense spending spree. Instead, he employed defense spending and the resulting budget deficits as a club with which to prod the Congress into cutting spending on social programs. The Congress would have had to virtually eliminate most social programs to accomodate the sharply higher defense spending and achieve a balanced budget. Its refusal to go along with this unrealistic scheme was utilized by Reagan to blame the Congress for the budget deficits.

Because of the improved relationship with the Soviet Union, the Bush Administration has decided to make some reductions in defense spending. For example, President Bush stated that the armed forces can be cut by twenty-five percent over the next five years (*Wall Street Journal*, August 3, 1990). However, it would be mistaken to interpret this statement as indicating a readiness to cut defense spending by $75 billion a year (25 percent of $300 billion). The President wants to develop expensive new weapons systems which would make cuts of this magnitude unlikely. I would estimate that the Bush Administration objective is to cut defense spending by no more than $50 billion annually by the fifth year.

In view of the fact that during the Reagan-Bush era defense spending was not properly funded, any reduction of less than $100 billion annually should be paid for with increased taxes. A realistic approach to funding defense spending is an essential precondition to balancing the budget.

To paraphrase the bible, "there is a time to arm, and a time to disarm." We have reached a point in history when drastic cuts in defense spending are in the best interest of the nation.

Questions and Answers

1. Why is Japan spending so little on defense?
Answer: The low defense spending policy was imposed on Japan by the U.S. after the Second World War. It was designed to prevent Japan from becoming a future threat to U.S. security. By faithfully adhering to this condition, the Japanes devoted their energies to peaceful pursuits and became an economic superpower. At the same times, they have relied on the U.S. to take care of their security needs, a service which the U.S. has supplied virtually free of charge. From a financial and economic standpoint, it was a fantastic deal for Japan and a disastrous one for the U.S.

2. What changes would you propose in this arrangement?

Answer: We should negotiate a fairer deal. The U.S. should spend less on defense and Japan should contribute more.

3. Wouldn't such a change involve the risk of Japan becoming a new threat to U.S. security and to other nations?

Answer: The Japanese government and people have learned from firsthand experience that peace is far more profitable than war. It is unlikely that they would jeopardize their wealth and prosperity with military adventurism. In any case, we should make sure that Japan agrees to policies that will not endanger U.S. military security.

4. Wouldn't sharp cuts in defense spending reduce U.S. influence in the world?

Answer: If we cut defense spending to $200 billion annually, we would still lead the rest of the world by a wide margin. Moreover, our influence in the world will be measured more by our financial condition and economic performance than by our military might. The record shows that our excessive defense spending has dissipated our wealth and undermined our economy. We would be far better off reducing our military expenditures and dedicating our efforts to restoring soundness to the government's finances and wholesomeness to the economy.

5. You criticize Reagan's tactics in using defense spending and the resulting deficits to get his way with Congress on budget matters. Don't you think it was necessary to curb the inclination of the Congress to spend too much on social programs?

Answer: A president has every right to state his budget preferences and to fight for them in an open and honest manner. However, he has no right to dictate to Congress on budget matters, or to use deceptive tactics to get his way. He should not have deliberately engineered budget deficits to accomplish his objectives.

6. *What should he have done?*

Answer: He should have told the American people that in his judgment we needed to increase defense spending sharply. His personal preference would be to pay for the defense buildup by reducing spending on social programs. However, if that approach could not be worked out with the Congress, he would have to propose tax increases. This procedure would have been in line with his commitment to a balanced budget.

7. *Reagan thought he could accomplish all of his goals, including a balanced budget, by stimulating economic growth which would result in higher federal revenues. You seem to ignore his economic philosophy, which was the basis for his policies.*

Answer: The record shows that his economic theories did not work out the way he had hoped they would. How many years of triple-digit deficits does one need to know that an approach is not working? He was told by his own Budget Director (David Stockman) and by others that his policies would produce chronically high deficits. Reagan's ideology and his advisors apparently blinded him from reality. The bottom line is that Reagan refused to fund defense spending in a responsible manner.

8. *It seems inconceivable that Reagan would propose $150 billion annual tax increases to pay for the defense buildup. Wouldn't he have had difficulty raising that much money?*

Answer: Reagan gave top priority to the defense buildup. Therefore, he should have been prepared to take the challenge of funding this program with appropriate revenue increases. This procedure would have had the advantage of providing strong incentives by his Administration, the Congress, and the American people to examine more carefully the magnitude of this spending and its necessity. It is possible, even likely, that if the full impact of this spending had been felt in our pocketbooks, it might have been scaled down somewhat and run with less waste and corruption. Moreover, we might have looked more closely at the purposes of this program, which might have led us to question the obsolete policy of subsidizing affluent allies with our defense umbrella. Reagan's procedure of relying on borrowed funds to pay for the defense buildup was irresponsible and played a key role in causing our budget predicament.

Interview with Democrat

DEM: Doc, your views on defense spending make a lot of sense, but you are unrealistic in expecting Bush to go along with them.

Dr. O: Why is that?

DEM: The military-industrial complex is a major source of financial and political support for Bush. If he cuts defense spending drastically, he would lose much of that support. It might jeopardize his plans for 1992. He is too shrewd a politician to take such chances.

Dr. O: But Bush is popular with the people and defense spending is increasingly unpopular. Taking a stand for lower defense spending might gain Bush more votes than he would lose from the defense establishment.

DEM: In addition to political considerations, Bush also has a deeply held conviction in favor of a strong military posture. He likes to negotiate from a position of strength.

Dr. O: Even if we cut defense spending by $100 billion annually, we would still be the most powerful nation in the world. We would get all the respect we need from leaders of other nations, allies and adversaries alike.

DEM: You underestimate the psychological factors involved. In the international sphere, weapons and armies count for a great deal. Prestige is a function of excess, not of scarcity. If we cut our arsenals by $100 billion, we would lose prestige.

At least, that is how Bush would probably feel.

Dr. O: Our excessive defense spending has played a key role in the dissipation of our wealth. Don't you think Bush is concerned about that reality?

DEM: Not nearly as much as you seem to be. To Bush and his right-wing supporters, a strong military establishment is essential. They would rather continue present policies, even if it means huge budget deficits, than cut back on defense spending in any significant way.

Dr. O: Would the Democrats act differently if they won control of the White House?

DEM: I believe we would.

Dr. O: Would the Democrats cut defense spending by $100 billion annually?

DEM: I wouldn't want to specify any exact figures, but I believe it is a reasonable assumption that Democrats would cut defense spending more than Republicans.

Dr. O: Would the Democrats devote all of the savings from reduced defense spending to cut the budget deficit?

DEM: Not all, but some. Our constituencies have been grossly neglected by the Reagan and Bush Administrations. They would be entitled to some of the benefits from reduced defense spending.

Dr. O: Insofar as Democrats would divert savings from defense spending to social programs, they would not accomplish the goal of a balanced budget.

DEM: Doc, you are too much preoccupied with a balanced budget. If we got a peace dividend of $100 billion we wouldn't just hand it over to the U.S. Treasury for deficit reduction.

Dr. O: How much would you allocate for that purpose?

DEM: I don't really know, but it would be a fair amount.

Dr. O: Would you use $75 billion for deficit reduction and $25 billion for increased social spending?
DEM: If I were to make an educated guess, I should think it would more likely be the other way around.

Dr. O: You mean, you would devote only $25 billion to deficit reduction? That would leave us $75 billion short of our goal.
DEM: Your goal, not ours. We don't think that deficit reduction overrides all other issues. In any case, if we need additional funds for balancing the budget, we should get the rich to pay for most of it. They were the main beneficiaries of Reaganomics; they should be held responsible for cleaning up the mess.

Dr. O: How do you propose to achieve that objective?
DEM: My first choice would be an increase in the top income tax rates. It would be the fairest and simplest procedure.

Dr. O: I am sure the rich won't think so.
DEM: The Republicans were not concerned about our feelings when they starved social programs with their policies.

Dr. O: Coming back to defense spending, where would Democrats make most of the cuts?
DEM: We would place primary emphasis on reducing foreign bases. We would want to minimize defense spending that subsidizes affluent allies. We would also make major cuts in weapons systems that are unneeded in the current international environment. On the other hand, we would be inclined to keep most domestic bases intact and to spend more on conventional weapons, particularly those which are already in production.

Dr. O: If I understand you correctly, you would curtail U.S. involvement in foreign countries. You would also cut expensive new weapons systems. However, you would minimize cuts on domestic bases or conventional weapons. It looks as if you are trying to safeguard the jobs of your constituents.

DEM: What is wrong with that?

Dr. O: It might not add up to the best defense.

DEM: Doc, all spending by the government is influenced by politics. The Republicans want advanced weapons systems costing billions of dollars because their constituents get most of the profits. The Democrats prefer spending money in ways that benefit the common man, the ordinary soldier and the worker in defense plants.

Dr. O: I suppose it is difficult, if not impossible, to get the best defense for the least money.

DEM: That has always been the case. You might as well learn to live with that reality.

Interview with Republican

REP: As you know, President Bush has played a major role in improving the international climate so that defense spending cuts were made possible.

Dr. O: I agree that President Bush deserves credit for having done a good job on the diplomatic front.

REP: What you don't seem to realize is the President was so effective because he was negotiating from a position of strength. If we had been weak militarily, it is unlikely that our adversaries would have made so many concessions.

Dr. O: One could make a good case for stating that the new attitude and policies of the Soviet Union were caused by the poor shape of the Soviet economy and by the fact that communism had lost its appeal throughout Eastern Europe.

REP: When it comes to military matters, the Soviet leaders

are realists. The story is told that Stalin dismissed the importance of the Pope because he lacked military power. Even though the present Soviet leaders are no fans of Stalin, they probably hold similar views on military matters.

Dr. O: The Pope probably has greater influence on history than most secular rulers with the world's strongest armies. The Soviet experience shows that armies which lack faith in their mission are not very effective. In any case, it is likely that Soviet leaders would respect us just as much if we cut military spending to $200 billion annually.

REP: You may be engaging in wishful thinking. I believe we would be taking a big chance if we made such drastic cuts.

Dr. O: The Soviet Union and the nations of Eastern Europe are highly dependent on outside financing to help build up their economies. Most of these countries, including the Soviet Union, would like the U.S. to play a key role in their transformation to market economies. Unfortunately, our excessive defense spending has placed serious limitations on our ability to meet their needs. We spend so much of our capital on weapons that we have inadequate funds left over to take care of investment needs at home and abroad. It is noteworthy that the main supplier of capital to Eastern Europe is West Germany, which spends a much smaller portion of its GNP on defense than we do. Moreover, the West German government has readily agreed to cut its defense spending even more as part of the arrangement for German unification.

REP: Their situation is special, not comparable to ours.

Dr. O: From a financial and economic standpoint, their policy makes a great deal of sense. They have decided to become an arsenal of peace, while leaving it to others to be arsenals of war. They are laying the foundation for playing a major role in East European economies, while we waste our resources on building more weapons that serve no useful purpose in the current international environment.

REP: The funds we are spending on defense couldn't be simply converted into investments in Eastern Europe.

Dr. O: There is a close relationship between defense spending and the availability of capital for investment. If we cut defense spending by $100 billion annually, government borrowing would decline by that amount. As a result, interest rates would drop sharply, the Federal Reserve would be able to implement easy credit policies, and the private sector would be in a position to make substantially greater investments.

REP: Do you mean that by simply reducing defense spending, the government would release forces within the private sector to generate new investments, at home and abroad?

Dr. O: There is an inverse relationship between defense spending and a flourishing private sector. The more a nation devotes its financial, technological, and scientific resources to defense, the less is available for the private sector. The Soviet Union was a good illustration of a nation which devoted most of its resources to defense, while seriously neglecting the private sector. Its armed forces were those of a superpower, while its economy was that of an underdeveloped nation. Japan illustrates the other extreme. The Japanese spend only one percent of their GNP on defense and devote 99 percent to the private sector. As a result, they have emerged as a financial and economic superpower with a very modest defense establishment. The U.S. stands inbetween these extremes. We started out as the world's leading economic superpower, unchallenged by anybody. In the 1940's and thereafter, we went all-out to become the world's strongest military power. In the process, we seriously weakened our economic position. Unless we make decisive changes soon, we will end up as a military superpower with a second-rate economy. This transformation is particularly unfortunate at a time when the role of the military is becoming less important in global affairs, while the influence of private sector economics is increasing. It seems ironical that the world has learned to appreciate our tradition of peaceful economic development, while we have fallen into the trap of excessive militarism. We are out of step with the march of history.

REP: That is your opinion. Isn't it also true that defense spending provides millions of jobs, which would be sharply reduced if we followed your advice?

Dr. O: The private sector would create many new jobs in connection with its investments. These jobs would add to the creation of wealth, while defense-related jobs tend to dissipate wealth. In terms of classical economic theory, we have a clear choice between impoverishing ourselves through excessive defense spending and enriching ourselves through greater private investments.

REP: Doc, you're oversimplifying. The scenario you describe would unfold only if the savings on defense spending were totally applied to budget deficit reduction. This is unlikely. Politicians have all kinds of pet projects for spending the "peace dividend."

Dr. O: If President Bush took the initiative on this matter, he could probably prevail in having most of the lowered defense spending applied to deficit reduction. If he explained the realities involved to the American people, they would probably support him in this effort.

Chapter 6
Let's Raise the Gasoline Tax by $1 a Gallon

Currently gasoline taxes in the U.S. average thirty cents per gallon, of which the federal government collects nine cents. In contrast, our trading partners in Western Europe and the Far East levy gasoline taxes averaging $2 per gallon. Our low gasoline tax policy was developed during former times when the U.S. enjoyed self-sufficiency from domestic oil production. At the present time, we import about half of our oil requirements. The dependence on oil imports will grow even more in the future. This reality subjects the U.S. to the risks of oil price escalations and/or supply disruptions. A substantial increase in the gasoline tax would be an important step to reduce this vulnerability and to help solve other problems.

It is proposed that during the next five years we increase the gasoline tax by twenty cents annually. Each cent of gasoline tax would generate about $1 billion annual revenues. By the end of five years, the proposed tax would yield an estimated $100 billion, unadjusted for conservation. This tax is one of the best available options for reducing budget deficits. It would also strengthen energy security, help the environment, lower interest rates, and improve the foreign trade balance. Each dollar of gasoline tax would generate several dollars of benefits.

By phasing in the tax over a five year period, the affected parties would have the opportunity to make appropriate adjustments. Car owners could purchase more fuel-efficient vehicles. Automobile manufacturers could produce the types of vehicles which would be in greatest demand. The federal government could facilitate matters by making provisions for hardship cases and by helping the domestic petroleum industry, whose clean-burning compressed natural gas (CNG) should be exempt from the tax.

It is estimated that the proposed tax would reduce gasoline consumption by about four percent annually. By the end of five years, the reductions might total about 1.5 million barrels a day. Some of this reduction would be offset by the net growth in vehicles.

U.S. energy security would be improved even more if compressed natural gas (CNG) were exempt from fuel taxes. As a result, it seems possible that several million vehicles, primarily those owned by fleet operators, would switch to CNG. The implementation of this program might replace a million barrels of imported oil a day by the end of the decade.

Vehicles fueled with gasoline are major sources of carbon monoxide, nitrogen oxides, and reactive hydrocarbons. These harmful pollutants would be reduced if car owners switched to more fuel-efficient vehicles or to clean-burning CNG. Vehicles with dedicated natural gas engines can virtually eliminate carbon monoxide and reactive hydrocarbons and greatly reduce nitrogen oxide emissions. Overall, the proposed gasoline tax would have very beneficial consequences for the environment.

Gasoline tax revenues would have a salutary effects on the federal budget. By the fifth year, gross revenues would increase by $100 billion, less adjustments estimated at $20 billion. If the $80 billion were dedicated to deficit reduction, the government's borrowing requirements would be sharply reduced. The overall deficit reduction proposed in Chapter 7 (Option 3) would bring interest rates down to levels not seen in decades. All borrowers would benefit from this development. The federal government, which owes more than $3 trillion, might save as much as $50 billion in annual interest costs, which would further improve the budget. The private sectors, including individuals, corporations, and local government, owe about $7 trillion. Their annual interest savings might aggregate $100 billion. Savings on interest costs alone would offset the cost of the gasoline tax for many car owners.

Low interest costs would be particularly advantageous to all capital-intensive enterprises, including utilities, petroleum and chemical industries, real estate and construction, agriculture and mining, and producers of big ticket consumer products which usually involve financing, such as cars, furniture, and appliances. Banks and other financial institutions would also benefit from lower interest rates. These developments would have a positive impact on employment opportunities, which would help many car owners.

The automobile industry would be a main beneficiary from the proposed gasoline tax. Car owners would have strong incentives to switch to more fuel-efficient vehicles. The new car business, which is currently in a depressed state, would get a big boost from these anticipated consumer responses. Moreover, lower interest costs would facilitate financing of vehicles. The automobile industry's large capital investments would also benefit from lower interest costs. It is not far-fetched to conclude that the proposed gasoline tax increase would be the best thing that could happen to the automobile industry.

The domestic petroleum industry would be another major beneficiary from the gasoline tax. The reduction in interest costs would be of great value to this industry, which is very capital-intensive. Moreover, the vehicular market for compressed natural gas would experience an upsurge, which would create new business for natural gas producers, pipe lines, and distributors.

Oil and natural gas are produced by the same industry. Knowledgeable people have reached the conclusion that the energy future of the U.S. is no longer with oil, but with natural gas. The state of Texas is the largest U.S. producer of both oil and natural gas. The government of that state has implemented legislation that favors compressed natural gas over gasoline as a vehicular fuel. The leading people of that state, who are among the best informed on matters involving oil and natural gas, have recognized that the increased use of natural gas for vehicles is in their own and their state's best interest. A substantial tax on gasoline, from which compressed natural gas would be exempt, would be compatible with this orientation. Fortunately, the best interests of the petroleum producing states and that of the nation as a whole can be enhanced through the proposed gasoline tax.

The U.S. foreign trade balance would be significantly improved as a result of the proposed gasoline tax policy. Oil import reductions would range from an estimated 300,000 barrels a day during the first year to 1.5-2.0 million barrels a day in the fifth year (the higher figure would result from a significant switch to compressed natural gas). The savings on foreign exchange would depend on the price of oil, but they would be substantial. By strengthening energy security, the gasoline tax would also make possible other savings, notably on defense spending and oil storage programs, both of which could be reduced.

The reduction in interest costs, which would follow in the wake of the gasoline tax increase, would have positive consequences on the foreign trade balance. Lower interest rates would reduce the capital and operating costs of U.S. enterprises which participate in foreign trade. Hitherto, the high gasoline taxes levied by governments in Western Europe and Japan have given their exporters a great advantage over their U.S. counterparts, which were handicapped by the low gasoline tax, high interest rate policy of our government. In effect, high gasoline tax policies have economic consequences similar to export subsidies in relation to countries with low gasoline tax policies. If we implemented the proposed gasoline tax increase, we would greatly improve the ability of our exporters to compete in the international marketplace. In addition to raising our exports, we would also be able to produce goods for the domestic U.S. market at competitive prices, which would reduce our dependence on imports. This combination of higher exports and lower imports would probably result in a positive foreign trade balance sometime in the 1990's.

If the proposed gasoline tax were equally divided among

the approximatley 180 million vehicles in the U.S., it would cost each vehicle owner about $110 in the first year and $560 in the fifth year. The actual amount of the tax will depend on a number of variables, the most important of which is the fuel-efficiency of the vehicle. The greater the fuel efficiency, the lower the tax. This reality tends to favor affluent individuals, most of whom drive late-model vehicles with high fuel efficiency. In contrast, economically disadvantaged individuals tend to drive older cars, most of which are inefficient gas guzzlers. Assuming they drive similar distances, affluent car owners are likely to pay less gasoline tax than the national average, while their poor counterparts will pay more. This analysis indicates that something must be done to help the poor adjust to higher gasoline taxes.

I would propose the following solution to this problem. The federal government should set aside ten percent of its gasoline tax revenues during the first five years to help the poor acquire fuel-efficient vehicles. The amounts involved would be in the $25-30 billion range. It should be noted that the poor would probably pay more in gasoline taxes than they would get back in the form of subsidies. It would be a good bargain for the federal government. It would also be advantageous for the poor, who would get fuel-efficient vehicles on a basis they can afford. Their standard of living would improve and they would gain experience in dealing with financial institutions. Millions of people who are currently outside the mainstream of the economy would be integrated in closer association, which would benefit them and society as a whole. The automobile industry would be a major beneficiary of this arrangement, which would create new markets for fuel-efficient used vehicles and for lower-priced new vehicles. Because old gas-guzzlers are major sources of air pollution, this approach would also benefit the environment.

I have done research and writing about the U.S. energy problems since 1979. It soon became apparent to me that a substantial increase in the gasoline tax was an essential condition for strengthening energy security. My first published article on this topic appeared in the *New York Times* on April 1, 1984. My book *Gasoline Tax Advantages* came out in 1987. *Fortune* presented my views on the gasoline tax in its December 5, 1988 issue.

During the past two years, a gasoline tax increase has received significant support from influential individuals. I include in that list anyone who supports this policy, regardless of the amounts involved in their proposals.

The following individuals have gone on public record as favoring an increase in the gasoline tax: the former and present Chairmen of the Federal Reserve, Paul Volcker and Alan Greenspan; the Co-Chairmen of the National Economic Commission, Drew Lewis and Robert Strauss; investment bankers Peter Peterson and Felix Rohatyn; economists Paul McCracken (University of Michigan), Lester Thurow (M.I.T.), James Tobin (Yale), and Robert Solow (M.I.T.); and business executives Harold Poling (Ford Motor), Lee Iacocca (Chrysler), Colby Chandler (Eastman Kodak), Elwin Larson (Brooklyn Union Gas), and John Young (Hewlett-Packard). Favorable comments about the gasoline tax have appeared in the *New York Times, Washington Post, Business Week, Fortune, Economist,* and *New Republic.* Congressman Anthony C. Beilenson of California has introduced bills in the Congress to raise the gasoline tax. Chairman Dan Rostenkowski of the Ways & Means Committee has stated that a gasoline tax increase is his "first choice" as a means for reducing the budget deficit (*New York Times,* December 7, 1988).

The American people are accustomed to accepting scientific and technical innovations fairly quickly. In contrast, they are extremely reluctant to embrace new concepts for solving social, economic, or government problems. For example, millions of computers have been installed in factories, offices, and homes. Hundreds of books have been written about computers and many periodicals have appeared devoted to this topic. In contrast, my book *Gasoline Tax Advantages* remains the only work on this issue, and it sold fewer than five thousand copies. Making allowance for my bias, I believe one can demonstrate that under present conditions the implementation of the proposed gasoline tax increase would have such a profoundly positive effect on our nation that its value would at least equal, if not surpass, that of the computer. The gasoline tax is an invaluable invention that can help the nation solve major energy, environmental, and financial problems at the lowest possible cost. It is the best energy tax.

Questions and Answers

1. Why not tax all forms of energy, rather than just gasoline?

Answer: Because gasoline is primarily responsible for our heavy dependence on oil imports and it is harmful to the environment. It would be senseless to tax natural gas, which is available from plentiful domestic sources, and which is environmentally beneficial. The gasoline tax would help the environment, strengthen energy security, and bring large revenues to the government. In contrast, a tax on natural gas or other clean domestic fuels would be counterproductive.

2. What do you think of an oil import tax?

Answer: An oil import tax is a disguised price-propping scheme. It would raise domestic oil and natural gas prices by the amount of the tax. It would cause inflationary pressures. It would raise interest rates. It would weaken U.S. exports. It would harm the economy. It would have negative conse-quences on long-term energy security (it would drain the U.S. of its remaining oil resources more quickly). It would worsen the federal budget deficit. It would do great harm to the international oil companies. It would undermine U.S. relations with oil exporting countries. It would have a negative multiplier effect, with harmful consequences far exceeding the benefits. A levy on oil imports is the worst energy tax. My book *Gasoline*

Tax Advantages contains more complete information on this topic.

3. Wouldn't the gasoline tax reduce consumer purchasing power?

Answer: The gasoline tax would set in motion a series of developments that would actually *increase* consumer purchasing power over time. As has been shown, reduced interest expenses in the private sector may offset the cost of the gasoline tax. The improved performance of U.S. participants in the international marketplace would mean more jobs for Americans and better profits for business. Similar consequences are likely to occur in such major industries as automobile manufacturing and natural gas production. All capital-intensive enterprises would benefit from lower interest rates. Overall, lower interest costs and better job opportunities would add more to the purchasing power of the average car owner than the cost of the gasoline tax. Moreover, owners of vehicles have the option to reduce the gasoline tax by purchasing more fuel-efficient vehicles.

4. If most people buy more fuel-efficient vehicles, wouldn't the federal gasoline tax revenues by reduced?

Answer: We are assuming a four percent annual reduction in gasoline consumption from existing vehicles, which would be partly offset by the growth in vehicles. Therefore, some reduction in gasoline tax revenues would be likely; it would probably be no more than ten percent from unadjusted figures. The rate of conversion to more fuel-efficient vehicles is the main variable determining the outcome. It this trend is greater than anticipated, the federal government would collect more taxes from the profits of automobile manufacturers and higher wages of their employees, which would make up in part or in whole the reduced revenues from the gasoline tax.

5. Does the U.S. have sufficient natural gas resources to take care of traditional markets as well as millions of vehicles fueled with CNG?

Answer: The U.S. currently uses about 19 trillion cubic feet (Tcf) of natural gas annually. According to studies by the American Gas Association, one Tcf of natural gas would supply enough fuel to power eight million vehicles for a year. Conventional natural gas resources in the U.S. are estimated at 983 Tcf, or about fifty times current annual consumption. Nonconventional sources of methane, the principal ingredient of natural gas, are many times as large as the conventional sources. In fact, methane can be produced from garbage, sewage, and energy crops, which will be available for as long as the sun shines and human beings inhabit the earth. The natural gas industry would have no problem supplying compressed natural gas to millions of vehicles. Readers who want a more comprehensive treatment of this topic are referred to my recently published book, *Natural Gas, the Best Energy Choice*.

6. Aren't there technical problems with using natural gas for powering vehicles?

Answer: Natural gas and oil are chemically very similar. In fact, natural gas can be used in engines fueled with gasoline or diesel with relatively few modifications. The equipment for making these changes is readily available from a number of sources. However, the full benefits of natural gas can be achieved only with a dedicated natural gas engine. Natural gas has an octane rating of 130, much higher than the 98 top for even the best gasoline. Dedicated natural gas engines are already available for buses and trucks.

The biggest obstacle to wider use of CNG for vehicles is financial, not technical. CNG filling stations require a compressor (to compress the gas) rather than the pumps which are used for liquid fuels. Currently, CNG filling stations are largely confined to the premises of gas utilities and some fleet operators, who service their own vehicles. Such filling stations are likely to cost $100,000 or more. Moreover, until demand for CNG powered vehicles picks up, manufacturers will not make the investments involved in building vehicles with dedicated natural gas engines. The proposed exemption of CNG from the gasoline tax would overcome these financial barriers.

7. What are the main obstacles to implementing the proposed gasoline tax increase?

Answer: Resistance to change and ignorance are the main barriers to the gasoline tax increase. For the past century, Americans have been accustomed to low gasoline taxes, which coincided with self-sufficiency in oil. However, current realities no longer justify this approach. We are now importing about fifty percent of our oil requirements, and this dependence on imported oil is stedily increasing. Under these circumstances, a substantial gasoline tax is essential to reduce wasteful consumption of energy. If U.S. vehicles had the same average fuel efficiency as their counterparts in Western Europe, we could reduce gasoline consumption by more than two million barrels a day. In fact, this figure is very similar to the goal we hope to achieve with the proposed gasoline tax increase.

For over a hundred years, the U.S. petroleum industry has focused primary attention on oil and such products as gasoline and diesel fuel. Natural gas was largely viewed as a byproduct of oil production. As a result of this orientation, our higher-grade, lower cost oil resources have been largely depleted. The average cost of finding new oil in the U.S. has been estimated at $15 a barrel. Considering the risks involved in oil exploration, high oil prices on a sustained basis are required to justify increased drilling activity. In contrast, economically attractive natural gas resources are still available in the U.S., even without a big jump in energy prices. Therefore, it makes good sense to place greater emphasis on natural gas as the major petroleum fuel in the U.S. While leaders of the oil industry have recognized the advantageous economics of natural gas, they have not as yet fully embraced the consequences of this reality. If they want to sell more natural gas, they must allow this fuel to enter new markets, including those currently monopolized by gasoline and diesel fuel in vehicular applications. For the sake of the nation, as well as in their own best self-interest, it is to be hoped they will soon embrace higher gasoline taxes and a more prominent role for natural gas in the vehicular market.

Interview with Democrat

Dr. O: How would Democrats respond to the proposed gasoline tax increase?

DEM: We wouldn't be very happy about it. First of all, we wouldn't like the regressive nature of the tax, most of which would be paid by our constituents. Secondly, among the leaders of the Democratic Party are senators and congressmen from energy-producing states, who have traditionally been opposed to a gasoline tax increase. Thirdly, we believe that if we are going to increase the gasoline tax, most of the proceeds should be used for improving the highway system and mass transit, not deficit reduction.

Dr. O: My proposal to set aside ten percent of the gasoline tax to help the poor acquire fuel-efficient vehicles was designed to reduce the regressive nature of the gasoline tax.

DEM: I recognize your good intentions, but you only take care of the extreme cases, not the great number of middle class people who have a hard time making ends meet and to whom a $560 increase in the gasoline tax would be a significant burden.

Dr. O: But they would also gain important benefits, including low interest costs and better job opportunities, which in most cases would more than offset the cost of the gasoline tax.

DEM: Most people won't look at it that way. They will see the higher gasoline prices very clearly, while the benefits are hidden and may not be readily linked in their minds to higher gasoline taxes.

Dr. O: This problem can be overcome through information and education.

DEM: That may be, but it still leaves the question unanswered as to why our constituents should carry the main burden of balancing the federal budget.

Dr. O: Actually, I also propose increased taxes specifically designed to make the rich pay their fair share, including higher income taxes and a levy on luxury purchases. The overall package for balancing the federal budget, including tax increases, is described in the last chapter of the book.

DEM: If the gasoline tax is part of an overall package, it becomes more acceptable. However, I still feel that our constituents will be paying a disproportionate share of the total.

Dr. O: It is unrealistic to look at the gasoline tax merely in terms of its impact on various categories of users. As you know, we are dependent on oil imports, which are steadily increasing. The politics of international oil are not favorable to the U.S. in general or to the interests of your constituents in particular. The price of gasoline has gone up by more than a dollar a gallon since the 1970's. Most of this increase benefited foreign producers. The full cost was born by U.S. vehicle owners, including the middle class and the poor. There were no offsetting benefits to your constituents or to the federal government. In fact, because of unsound energy policies, we were burdened with high inflation rates, high interest costs, and recessions, all of which victimized your constituents. You shouldn't allow your preoccupation with tax fairness to blind you to these broader realities.

DEM: I must admit that you make some convincing arguments in favor of the proposed gasoline tax increase. But you should remember that most politicians and their constituents

116

don't have this broad perspective. They focus primarily on the immediate results, which don't look good to them.

Dr. O: You mean most Americans would rather be exploited by foreign oil producers than pay taxes to their own government?
DEM: We have no control over foreign oil producers, but we have leverage over our elected officials.

Dr. O: You stated at the beginning that some influential Democrats in the Congress oppose a gasoline tax increase because they fear it would have adverse consequences for energy producers in their states. This orientation is basically flawed. As long as the U.S. was self-sufficient in oil, energy producing states had a vested interest in keeping gasoline consumption high and avoiding taxes on energy products. However, under present circumstances, the main beneficiaries of our low gasoline tax policy are foreign oil producers, not domestic ones. Moreover, I propose that compressed natural gas (CNG), which comes from plentiful domestic sources, be exempt from the gasoline tax. As a result domestic petroleum producers would become major beneficiaries from the proposed gasoline tax increase. If member of Congress from the energy-producing states had a proper understanding of these realities, they should be in the vanguard of those leading the Congress to approving the gasoline tax increase.
DEM: Have you tried communicating with these people?

Dr. O: I have tried, but I haven't been very successful.
DEM: Why not?

Dr. O: I don't know. In all probability, my communications weren't even read by the people to whom they were addressed. Their staff members probably assumed that their principals would not be interested in seeing any letters favoring a gasoline tax increase.

DEM: Maybe we should arrange appearances by you before appropriate congressional committees to discuss this issue. Would you be prepared to make such appearances?

Dr. O: I would be glad to cooperate with the Congress on this matter.

DEM: Hitherto, the gasoline tax has been utilized for highway construction and repair. In view of the poor shape of many highways, we believe some of the gasoline tax increase should be used for this purpose. Similarly, many Democrats feel that the federal government should play a more active role in helping to improve mass transit, which is in a pitiful condition in many parts of the country. The gasoline tax would be an appropriate source for funding this program.

Dr. O: There is little doubt that we need to improve highways and mass transit. However, if we use a substantial part of the gasoline tax to finance those programs, we will interfere with achieving the objective of balancing the budget. Fortunately, we may have an alternative option.

DEM: What is that?

Dr. O: As we will show in the last chapter, the deficit reduction package, including the gasoline tax increase, would result in sharply lower interest rates. As a result, capital-intensive activities, like highway and mass transit projects, would be much less costly to finance. They can be structured in a way to enable them to be self-supporting through modest user fees. It may even be possible to interest the private sector in financing some of these projects.

DEM: But that procedure would be a fundamental departure form existing practice.

Dr. O: That might not be such a bad thing, considering the fact that the results achieved with existing practices leave much to be desired.

DEM: Highways and mass transit are of major interest to politicians whose constituents will judge them to a considerable extent by how much they can accomplish in those areas.

Dr. O: The less politics in relation to highways and mass transit, the better.

DEM: If you remove the gasoline tax from financing highways and mass transit, you will greatly reduce the appeal of that tax to politicians.

Dr. O: The time has come for politicians to look beyond their usual parochial preoccupations and consider the national interest. All other industrial countries levy gasoline taxes substantially higher than the amount I am proposing for the U.S. Their governments have acted on the assumption that automobiles should make a substantial contribution to the economic cost of improved energy security. Our government has followed the opposite policy. We forced the general economy to subsidize the automobile. The results clearly indicate that our policy has been unsound and self-destructive. It is to be hoped that the American people and their representatives in government will finally learn this lesson and come out in favor of the proposed gasoline tax increase.

Interview with Republican

Dr. O: What do Republicans think of a gasoline tax increase?

REP: Most Republicans are opposed to all tax increases, including one on gasoline. They feel we should balance the budget solely through spending cuts.

Dr. O: That is a pipe dream. There is no way in which the real operating budget deficit of the government can be eliminated without substantial tax increases. In fact, even the reported budget deficit of $169 billion cannot be brought under control without tax increases, as President Bush has acknowledged.

REP: The American people aren't clamoring for a gasoline tax increase.

Dr. O: Support for a gasoline tax increase has become fairly substantial. A poll conducted by the Wall Street Journal/NBC News showed that 38% of those interviewed favored a gasoline tax increase (*Wall Street Journal,* July 12, 1990).

REP: But 59% were opposed, which is still a substantial majority.

Dr. O: If the American people were properly informed about the gasoline tax, support for such action would grow. My own experience supports this conclusion. I have given several lectures on the gasoline tax. I started out by asking my audience, most of whom were businessmen, how many would favor a gasoline tax increase of $1 per gallow. Virtually no one raised his hand. Then I explained the advantages of the gasoline tax, as spelled out in this chapter. When I asked the audience at the end of my lecture how many favored a gasoline tax increase, the majority signified approval. Unfortunately, I can only reach a small number of people. If President Bush were to announce his support for such action, most Americans would support him.

REP: I am sure President Bush has no intention of coming out in favor of a gasoline tax increase.

Dr. O: Why not?

REP: As you know, the President was strongly opposed by most members of our party when he endorsed the idea of tax increases as part of the deficit reduction package. He cannot afford to lose additional political capital by supporting an unpopular tax like that on gasoline. We would rather focus on raising taxes on alcohol and tobacco, which have strong popular support.

Dr. O: Increasing top income tax rates also ranks high in popularity with the American people.

REP: We oppose such a measure.

Dr. O: In effect, you don't hesitate to oppose popular taxes if they are against the interests of your support groups. Why shouldn't you support a tax that helps the nation as a whole, including your own constituents?

REP: Not all of our constituents would benefit from a gasoline tax increase.

Dr. O: Who wouldn't?

REP: The petroleum industry, for example.

Dr. O: My gasoline tax proposal is structured in such a way that the petroleum industry would be a major beneficiary. All sectors of that capital-intensive industry would be helped by the lower interest rates which would follow in the wake of a substantial gasoline tax increase. In addition, the proposed exemption of compressed natural gas (CNG) from any fuel tax would give a big boost to the domestic market for natural gas.

REP: Doc, there are some fundamental issues involved in this matter which you seem to ignore.

Dr. O: What fundamental issues?

REP: You are ignoring the impact of a substantial gasoline tax increase on the oil industry's control over prices. Look, a $1 per gallon gasoline tax translates into $42 per barrel. There is just so much money to be made on a barrel of oil. If the government takes a big bite in the form of a gasoline tax, there is little room for oil producers and gasoline refiners to raise their prices. A big gasoline tax would stifle the oil industry.

Dr. O: Other industrial countries levy gasoline taxes averaging $2 per gallon, or $84 per barrel. The oil industry still makes good profits in those countries.

REP: Those profits are less satisfactory than you may think. In any case, the U.S. is the largest market for gasoline and a big fuel tax would harm the vital interests of the petroleum industry.

Dr. O: What vital interests?

REP: It would hamper their ability to raise prices. Just imagine what $100 billion would do to revitalize the domestic energy industry.

Dr. O: You mean, the oil industry should have the right to tax the American people on gasoline, not the federal government?

REP: The oil industry doesn't levy taxes; its concern is with prices. Taxes interfere with the economic freedom to set prices that maximize return on investment. That is what free enterprise is all about. Isn't that what Adam Smith meant when he said "the unseen hand of the marketplace" should determine prices?

Dr. O: What you have described sounds more like "the grasping claws of the greedy monopolists." If you read *The Wealth of Nations,* you will find that Smith strongly opposed monopolistic pricing practices. They are the antithesis of the free market.

REP: But wouldn't Adam Smith also have opposed the gasoline tax increase?

Dr. O: Not at all. Under present circumstancs, Adam Smith would have been a strong supporter of a substantial gasoline tax increase. He would have been horrified at our huge budget deficits and public debt. He would have advocated any realistic actions to cope with these problems. Furthermore, Adam Smith had a profound grasp of the interrelationships among economic forces. He would have seen that the low gasoline tax policy

122

placed the U.S. at a serious disadvantage in the international marketplace.

REP: Doc, there is another matter which you overlook when you compare gasoline with compressed natural gas (CNG). The petroleum industry is fully integrated in the oil business. The big companies produce the oil, transport it, refine it, and sell it in filling stations. In contrast, they only produce the natural gas, while they are legally constrained from owning gas pipelines or distribution companies.

Dr. O: Maybe we should lift those constraints.

REP: You mean, we should allow oil companies to enter gas transportation and distribution activities?

Dr. O: Provided the interests of existing gas companies are safeguarded, it would make sense to allow oil companies to distribute compressed natural gas to end consumers.

REP: How would that work?

Dr. O: If compressed natural gas is to become a major factor in the transportation sector, an infrastructure of thousands of filling stations would have to be established. The most logical and least costly locations would be on the sites of existing gasoline stations, many of which are already connected to natural gas. The oil industry should be encouraged to construct such facilities.

REP: That would involve spending billions of dollars.

Dr. O: That is correct. But they would be compensated by creating a new market for natural gas, one that would be highly profitable to them. It would also help solve major energy and environmental problems.

REP: You seem to support more profits for the oil industry in connection with natural gas and less for their gasoline business.

Dr. O: Profits should be earned by fulfilling a vital function for customers and for society as a whole. Expanding the market for compressed natural gas meets this criterion. On the other hand, condoning monopolistic pricing policies in relation to gasoline is not in the best interest of consumers or the nation.

REP: Doc, you are too moralistic about economic issues. That is not what classical economics is all about.

Dr. O: On the contrary, that is exactly the viewpoint of classical writers on economics. For example, Adam Smith was a professor of moral philosophy at Glasgow University. He saw a close link between economics and ethics.

REP: In terms of political realism, the oil industry holds the key to any substantial gasoline tax increase. If you can convince them that such a tax could be structured in a way to promote their vital interests, they might give it serious consideration. But I wouldn't be too optimistic on that score. They have a strong tradition of opposition to government interference in their affairs and to any energy taxes. All you have to offer is some innovative ideas, while they possess plenty of cash and political clout.

Dr. O: An idea whose time has come can be more powerful than cash and political influence. I hope we can persuade leaders of the oil industry and President Bush to support the gasoline tax, which is the best available option for solving many of our problems.

DEM: That seems to be the view almost universally held by most of the people I know, not only politicians but also economists and the media.

Dr. O: Since the 1930's, we have had virtually uninterrupted deficits. It is difficult for anyone to envisage what would happen if we had a prolonged period of balanced budgets.

DEM: We know from the history prior to the 1930's that the economy experienced ups and downs while the budget was balanced.

Dr. O: We have had business cycles since the 1930's as well.

DEM: But they were less severe than those that occurred previously.

Dr. O: The deficits may have cushioned the severity of the cycles, though that is by no means a certainty. However, this policy loaded the government down with an enormous debt, which now exceeds $3,000 billion. Prior to the New Deal, the government was practically free of debt. In fact, the deficit spending policies of the New Deal were made possible by the strong financial condition of the government. We are no longer in that position.

DEM: Government debt does not need to bother us as long as the economy continues to perform well.

Dr. O: But we cannot assume that this condition will prevail much longer. The financial and economic distortions created by the budget mismanagement in recent years could result in a serious predicament. We might get a severe recession at a time the government would be ill prepared to deal with it.

DEM: What would happen?

Dr. O: We would have to fight a recession while trying to restore soundness to the government's finances. It would be a complex challenge, one that could not be met merely by

143

applying the approach that was used in the 1930's and subsequent economic downturns.

DEM: You mean, we couldn't solve the problem with more deficit spending?

Dr. O: That is the way I see it. In my opinion, the proposals outlined in Option 3 are the best available means for coping with any recession that might come our way.

DEM: But wouldn't we run the risk of precipitating a recession by taking such drastic steps to balance the budget?

Dr. O: In my opinion, we are going to have a recession, no matter what we do or avoid doing. The coming recession reflects financial and economic forces that have been building over the past decade of excessive stimulation. The best policy would be to stop worrying about what may trigger the recession and start taking actions that would put the government's financial house in order. Sharply reduced government borrowing will bring down interest rates, which will stimulate the economy. It is our best available option.

DEM: How do you know this approach will work?

Dr. O: Because it makes good economic sense. If interest rates drop sharply enough on a sustained basis, the private sector will generate sufficient capital spending to bring about the desired results.

DEM: In most recessions capital spending declines. What would make it different this time?

Dr. O: In previous recessions the government added to deficit spending, which signaled higher interest rates in the future. Under Option 3, deficit reduction by the government would create conditions for lowering interest rates on a long-term basis, which is essential for encouraging major capital investments.

DEM: We have had no experience with that approach.

144

Unforeseen problems could arise which might place it in jeopardy.

Dr. O: The chances we would be taking would be far smaller than those that would accompany a continuation of our present policies.

DEM: People in government and in the private sector are not accustomed to thinking along those lines.

Dr. O: Fear of the unknown is understandable, but it need not be an insurmountable obstacle. As a general rule, any time a nation positions itself to create and accumulate wealth, positive forces are likely to emerge that would move the economy forward. The opposite happens when a nation dissipates wealth, which has been our experience in recent years.

DEM: Democrats are in a quandary about these issues. We thought we were doing a reasonably good job with the economy since the 1930's. Admittedly, we had generated some budget deficits, but they were not excessive and posed no serious threat to the economy. Then Reagan came along with policies that created unprecedented deficits, which are clearly a threat to the government's finances and to the economy. We want to do what we can to reduce these deficits. But we also need to consider our constituencies, many of whom are in dire need of more assistance.

Dr. O: Who are your major constituencies?

DEM: The middle class and the poor.

Dr. O: Have these constituencies changed since the 1930's?

DEM: Not really.

Dr. O: But their situation is different today from what it was in the 1930's.

DEM: What do you mean?

Dr. O: In the 1930's, most people in the middle class were poor. That is not the case currently.

DEM: It is true that the middle class has more wealth today than they did during the depression.

Dr. O: Much more. Let us consider this matter more closely. The total wealth of the U.S. has been estimated to exceed $30 trillion. About two-thirds of that wealth is owned by the rich. The other third is largely in the hands of the middle class. We are talking about $10 trillion. To place this sum in perspective, if it were equally divided among the 250 million Americans, everyone would get $40,000.

DEM: That is quite a lot of money. But what does it mean in terms of political realities?

Dr. O: It means that the middle class has a big stake in reducing budget deficits. A substantial part of the middle class wealth is directly linked to the government's finances. This comment is particularly applicable to trust funds for Social Security, government employees and railroad workers pension funds, and veterans life insurance, all of which are administered by the government.

DEM: You mean, if the government's finances experienced problems, the integrity of these trust funds might be placed in jeopardy?

Dr. O: That is right. One should be especially concerned about this matter because the trust fund surpluses are used by the government to understate the real scope of the budget deficits. It is a deceptive and dangerous game that should be stopped. Because most of the people involved in these programs are your constituents, the Democrats should take the lead in protecting these assets. The best procedure for accomplishing this goal is to balance the real operating budget, as proposed in Option 3.

DEM: If your analysis is correct, the Democrats would have

as strong a motivation as Republicans in bringing soundness to the government's finances.

Dr. O: That is the case. Moreover, the Democrats should take the lead in assuring the safety of the trust funds by insisting that the federal budget be balanced without using these funds to understate the true scope of the problem.

DEM: Many of our people feel that cutting the budget deficit by $169 billion over the next few years may be excessive. Your proposal would involved the elimination of a $380 billion deficit. Politically, that does not look feasible.

Dr. O: If the American people and their representatives in government set their minds to it, we can accomplish this goal.

DEM: You are proposing a complete change in thinking, particularly for the Democrats.

Dr. O: Hitherto, the Democrats have largely ignored the substantial wealth of the middle class. As a result, they have assumed that deficits would not harm their constituents very much, if at all. Now you discover that your constituents may be among the main victims of the deficits.

DEM: But the rich have even more to lose than the middle class. They control the other two-thirds of the wealth, or some $20 trillion.

Dr. O: The representatives of the rich and the middle class, meaning Republicans and Democrats, should work together to eliminate the budget deficits and create the conditions for wealth creation and accumulation.

DEM: Where does that leave the poor, who are our other major constituency?

Dr. O: Both political parties should share responsibility for helping the poor. It is unrealistic and unfair to place the whole burden on the Democrats and blame them for everything that goes wrong with social spending.

DEM: But that would mean we would no longer have the popular vote that makes us the majority party.

Dr. O: There would be more competition between Republicans and Democrats for the votes of the poor, but that would be all to the good. It would help the poor, which would be the main objective.

DEM: I don't think the Democrats would like this approach.

Dr. O: The Republicans resent spending on social programs because they feel the Democrats get all the credit and most of the votes, while the Republicans pay a sustantial part of the bills. Why not let the Republicans sponsor and administer some of these programs? At the least, they won't be able to blame the Democrats if things go wrong. It would be a good experience for them.

DEM: But they would get votes that are currently Democratic.

Dr. O: They would have to earn those votes through responsible behavior. At the same time, it would relieve the Democrats of excessive responsibilities which they cannot properly discharge in the foreseeable environment. The best interests of the poor should be placed ahead of political considerations.

DEM: You are asking more of politicians than they are prepared to do. I doubt that the Democrats would give up their constituencies among the poor without a major fight.

Dr. O: It would be a good thing if Republicans and Democrats fight for the allegiance of the poor. Whoever does the best job, deserves to win.

DEM: Our discussions have gone far afield from the original topic of balancing the budget.

Dr. O: We have seen that the budget is at the heart of government and of politics.

DEM: If what you are saying is true, then both political parties are likely to be fundamentally transformed in the next few years.

Dr. O: That is a reasonable assumption.

DEM: But who will win the next election?

Dr. O: That will depend on how the budget problem would be handled by the respective parties.

DEM: Historically, Republicans have had the advantage on budget matters.

Dr. O: That may no longer be the case. If the Democrats recognize that their stake in a balanced budget is as great as that of the Republicans, they might support policies that would keep the middle class in their fold and that may even attract many people who have previously voted Republican.

DEM: You mean people who might be disenchanted with the legacy left by Reagan's budget policies?

Dr. O: Precisely.

DEM: Don't underestimate the Republicans if they are backed into a corner. For example, it wouldn't surprise me if they took up your suggestion to solve the savings and loan fiasco by putting a surcharge on estate taxes. From a partisan standpoint, I hope they won't accept your recommendation. The Democrats believe that the savings and loan mess will be one of their strong hands in the 1992 election.

Dr. O: But it would make a major contribution to solving the budget problem.

DEM: We could take care of that matter after we got into the White House.

Dr. O: I have presented all of my recommendations for balancing the budget on an impartial, non-partisan basis. Both political parties have the opportunity to make use of these ideas as they see fit.

DEM: I am aware of that fact. But the savings and loan bailout recommendation would favor the Republicans more than the Democrats.

Dr. O: The Republicans would pay most of the cost.

DEM: But it might enable them to win an election they would otherwise lose.

Dr. O: There will undoubtedly be many other issues in that campaign.

DEM: None as graphic as the savings and loan mess.

Dr. O: I would like to see both political parties give top priority to the achievement of a balanced budget. The survival of the nation depends on the transformation from wealth dissipation to wealth creation and accumulation.

DEM: If enough Americans want to achieve these goals, the Democrats will respond favorably.

Interview with Republican

REP: Doc, your Option 3 presents some interesting ideas, but it violates a fundamental principle of politics.

Dr. O: What is that principle?

REP: That one should avoid drastic departures from existing policies.

Dr. O: Even if those policies are fundamentally flawed, dissipate the nation's wealth and jeopardize its most vital interests.

REP: That is correct.

Dr. O: Are you saying that if our nation is moving in the wrong direction, it is doomed?

REP: Not quite. Our political system provides for some flexibility. For example, Option 2, which describes the deficit reduction proposal being considered by the Bush Administration and the Congress, falls within the range of acceptable behavior.

Dr. O: But Option 2 is grossly inadequate.

REP: That may be, but it is politically as far as we can go. In fact, the parties involved in the negotiations are finding it very difficult to work out an acceptable deficit reduction package. Can you imagine the wrangling that would be going on to eliminate a budget deficit more than twice as large as the $169 billion currently under discussion?

Dr. O: The $380 billion real operating budget deficit is an objective fact. It isn't something to be manipulated by politicians into an "acceptable" framework, to suit their purposes.

REP: You are wrong. The most important task of politicians is to define the problem in such a way that it appears to be manageable. Then they can go to the voters and claim credit for having solved the predicament.

Dr. O: You mean politics is a game of make-believe, in which facts are restructured in such a way that politicians can look good to the voters?

REP: Precisely. You have ignored this fundamental reality of politics. Therefore, Option 3 has no chance of implementation.

Dr. O: But isn't it important for the American people and their representatives in government to know what the real problems are and how they can be solved?

REP: It may have some positive consequences, but it also has some risks.

Dr. O: What are the positive consequences?

REP: It may act like a compass, which would help politicians to see whether they are moving in the right direction. It may also provide some useful ideas which might be incorporated into their deficit reduction program.

Dr. O: What are the risks?

REP: If many people demand the actions you propose, it would make it more difficult for politicians to act in accustomed ways. It might even influence elections, which no politician likes unless it works in his favor.

Dr. O: But they could readily achieve that objective by embracing Option 3.

REP: You fail to see that many voters would not like some or all of your recommendations. For example, how many voters would favor a gasoline tax of $1 per gallon?

Dr. O: Most realistic, fair-minded individuals would support a gasoline tax increase as part of a deficit reduction package designed to balance the budget and to achieve other important objectives, like energy security.

REP: How many voters are realistic and fair-minded? You are talking about a small minority. Most voters look at taxes in terms of the impact on their own pocketbooks, not on the basis of what they would do to solve the nation's problems.

Dr. O: If democracy is to function, the citizens must act responsibly in relation to government affairs, particularly if survival issues are involved.

REP: That may be fine in theory, but politicians have to deal in practicalities. Unless there is a groundswell of public support for Option 3, politicians will have to assume that it is irrelevant to the practical matters with which they are concerned.

Dr. O: But if we don't implement Option 3, we are likely to face a crisis some time in the future.

REP: We will deal with the crisis if and when it comes.

Dr. O: Don't politicians believe in preventing trouble before it arises?

REP: They have plenty of current troubles to deal with. They are not going to conern themselves with future problems that may not occur until after they leave office.

Dr. O: I can understand why you don't hold out much hope for Option 3.

REP: Nevertheless, some of your ideas may be incorporated in the political process.

Dr. O: Which ones?

REP: Your most original suggestion concerns the handling of the savings and loan bailout.

Dr. O: You think the proposal to eliminate the savings and loan problem by levying a surcharge on estate taxes has merit?

REP: My first reaction was quite negative, because you are suggesting that Republicans should pay most of the surcharge.

Dr. O: You mean that people with estates of more than $100,000 are likely to be Republicans?

REP: The highest surcharge would be on estates of $1 million or more; those are primarily our constituents.

Dr. O: You believe that most millionaires are Republicans.

REP: They are if they know what's good for them. I realize there are some wealthy Democrats, but I have a suspicion there must be something wrong with them. Maybe they are masochists or feel guilty about having money.

Dr. O: My Democratic informants tell me they are idealists.

REP: In any case, the largest amount of the bailout would be paid by people with large estates.

Dr. O: I thought you said you found something positive about my recommendation.

REP: I assure you, it was not on financial grounds, because most of our people will be up in arms about it. However, politically it makes a lot of sense.

Dr. O: Why is that?

REP: Polls indicate that most voters have very negative reactions to the savings and loan bailout. In fact, they are furious about it. They don't want to pay any part of it. They feel it should be paid by the wrongdoers and others who benefited from it. As usual, their views are simplistic. In actuality only a small portion of the funds involved could be recovered from wrongdoers. Moreover, while both political parties are equally responsible for the fiasco, there is an unfair tendency to blame the Republicans more than the Democrats. Whenever you have a problem that involves large sums of money, people automatically assume that the Republicans are the main culprits. This viewpoint is of course nonsensical, but nevertheless, it has political reality which cannot be ignored. It could play a role in the 1992 election.

Dr. O: You mean a realistic resolution of the savings and loan bailout in the near future might help President Bush's chances for reelection in 1992?

REP: We would have to give the matter a lot of thought and test it out with our consultants and large contributors. We would want to examine the terms carefully to be certain they are fair and workable. We would also want to make sure that the levy on the estate taxes would be limited to the savings and loan bailout and that no further surcharges on estate taxes would be allowed for many years to come. We don't want to give the Democrats an opportunity to finance social programs with additional estate taxes. If these conditions are carefully spelled out, action along these lines may make good sense. The fact that most of the surcharge would be paid by very wealthy individuals would actually be a point in its favor from a political standpoint. It would probably go over well with the electorate.

Dr. O: It would be an important step in the direction of stopping the wealth dissipation.
REP: I am not sure about that.

Dr. O: Why not?
REP: Because the money the government takes from the estates won't be available for investment in the private sector, which is the engine of wealth creation.

Dr. O: But the savings and loan bailout is a festering wound which would harm the private sector for decades to come unless we do something along the lines suggested in Option 3.
REP: From an economic standpoint, most Republicans would disagree with you, but politically it makes a lot of sense.

Dr. O: Do any other proposals contained in Option 3 appeal to you?
REP: I like the suggestion to reduce waste in government by $50 billion annually. I would double that number and cut back less on defense spending.

Dr. O: Any defense spending in excess of necessity is also wasteful. In fact, it may do even more harm than spending in other areas, because defense spending is closely linked to the loss of U.S. assets to foreigners.
REP: We are not as concerned about the loss of assets to foreigners as you seem to be. Foreign investment stimulates our economy.

Dr. O: It also impairs our independence. I believe we should give top priority to eliminating this threat, particularly in view of the fact that it is based on our own irresponsible behavior in relation to the budget. Option 3 is the only realistic approach for restoring the U.S. to the role of net creditor to the rest of the world.

REP: As I stated before, you are expecting too much from voters and from politicians.

Dr. O: What do you think of Option 3 as a whole?

REP: It is heavily rigged against Republican constituencies.

Dr. O: You mean that my proposals would make the wealthy pay a substantial part of the costs involved in balancing the budget?

REP: Precisely. Why couldn't we cut more fat from social programs? If the Democrats insist on that type of spending, let them pay for it with taxes that are more evenhanded in their impact, like general consumption taxes.

Dr. O: My studies indicate that the current budget deficit was caused primarily by the defense build-up during the Reagan era, which was never funded with tax increases.

REP: Reagan wanted to pressure the Democrats to cut back on social spending. If he had raised taxes, the Democrats would have spent more on social programs.

Dr. O: Your comment is not very logical. If Reagan had paid for the defense spending increase, that would not have involved increasing social spending. He was using the unfunded defense spending for ulterior purposes, which played a key role in causing the budget predicament. It should be a basic principle to pay in full for any spending the government does, whatever the purpose of that spending.

REP: The Democrats had a big headstart with social spending. Reagan played catch-up with defense spending.

Dr. O: The Democrats did a reasonably good job of funding their spending programs as they were incurred. They didn't leave a legacy of triple-digit deficits.

REP: Democrats funded their programs by levying high taxes on our constituents. That is at the heart of the problem and why we resent the Democrats. They made Republicans pay for most of their programs.

Dr. O: The constituents of the Democratic Party represent the majority of the people, while the Republican minority has most of the wealth. It is logical that the wealthy should pay a larger share of the cost of government programs.

REP: But it is patently unfair. They get the credit and the votes, while we pay the bills.

Dr. O: Perhaps the Republicans should develop a different approach to running the government.

REP: What approach?

Dr. O: Instead of focusing on the supposed unfairness of social programs and their financing, why not play a positive role in structuring and administrating them? That way, waste and inefficiency would be reduced, which would lower their costs and taxes needed to pay for them. Moreover, with that approach Republicans would get more of the credit for these programs.

REP: Republicans would become a watered-down version of the Democrats if they followed that procedure.

Dr. O: Not necessarily. One can be conservative and socially responsible at the same time. Do you know who started social security legislation?

REP: Franklin Delano Roosevelt.

Dr. O: In the U.S., but that was long after it had been implemented in most European countries. Guess who sponsored

157

it there?

REP: Probably the Socialists or the Communists.

Dr. O: You are wrong. It was Prince Otto von Bismarck, the first Chancellor of Germany, a most conservative gentleman.

REP: Why would a conservative sponsor social security?

Dr. O: Because he felt that it was important for the common man to have basic economic security and to have a concrete stake in the nation. Such a policy would actually reduce the appeal of extremists.

REP: It may have worked for Germany, but in this country we got our share of extremism. The social legislation of the Democrats may well have the dubious distinction of leading the world. We are spending more on social programs than anybody else.

Dr. O: Not on a per capita basis. Most European countries spend much more on social programs than the U.S., inspite of the fact that their problems are less severe than ours.

REP: If they want to waste their money on social spending, that is their privilege. The Republicans are going to do their best to avoid falling into that trap.

Dr. O: Maybe it isn't a trap, but reality. Republicans would be well advised to look at these issues more objectively and with less emotionalism about the supposed unfairness involved.

REP: That is your opinion. In any case, it takes us far afield from dealing with the budget problem.

Dr. O: Not at all. The obsession of Reagan and many Republicans against spending on social programs has played a key role in causing our budget predicament. This orientation appeals to the emotions, but does little to solve the problem. An increase in social awareness and concern by Republicans would be a great boon to their party and the nation. Coping with social problems should no longer be the monopoly of the Democrats.

REP: Where would that leave the Democrats?

Dr. O: They should become more concerned about preserving and increasing the nation's wealth.

REP: You mean the Democrats should become more like the Republicans and vice versa?

Dr. O: Both political parties have a major stake in ridding the nation of the unsound budget policies that have caused the massive dissipation of our wealth. However, the Republicans have a special responsibility in this regard.

REP: Why is that?

Dr. O: Because your constituents control more of the nation's wealth than the Democrats.

REP: Do you mean that if Republicans act irresponsibly in relation to the budget, it is worse than if the Democrats do?

Dr. O: That is correct. In their own best self-interest, Republicans should give top priority to balancing the budget.

REP: Even if that means letting the Democrats get away with wasteful social spending?

Dr. O: Even then. For Republicans, balancing the real operating budget deficits, as defined in Option 3, should have top priority. There is no valid excuse for Republicans to depart from that principle for any reason.

REP: Your comment would imply that Republicans should take the initiative in balancing the budget.

Dr. O: Without a question.

REP: President Bush seems to be leaning in that direction.

Dr. O: He is not going far enough. The real Republican budget agenda for the 1990's should be the transformation from wealth dissipation to wealth accumulation, as spelled out in Option 3.

REP: You are saying this because you are infatuated with Option 3.

Dr. O: I am saying it because it is true.

REP: Tell me, Doc, why did you write this book?

Dr. O: Because I wanted to alert the American people to the dangers confronting the nation as a result of unsound budget policies, which have dissipated our wealth and jeopardized our democratic institutions and our independence.

REP: Are you sure you don't have ulterior motives, like wanting to become the next budget director or running for political office?

Dr. O: I have no such ambitions.

REP: Would you consult with the President, if he asked you?

Dr. O: Yes, I would.

REP: In relation to budget matters, do you have any preference between Republicans and Democrats?

Dr. O: I do not. The budget problem is so serious that it should be handled on a bipartisan basis.

REP: You have presented ideas that challenge sixty years of conventional wisdom. How can you be sure that you are right?

Dr. O: I have been actively involved in dealing with budget issues for many years, with particular emphasis on inflation, energy policy, and Reaganomics. It became increasingly clear to me that our budget policies were fundamentally flawed. They had counterproductive consequences. They caused the massive dissipation of wealth. They enriched foreigners at the expense of the American people. They violated the principles of classical economic theory. They were contrary to common sense and to rational behavior.

I believe I am on solid ground in challenging the conventional wisdom that has saddled the nation with these harmful policies for the past sixty years.

go much further. The implementation of this policy should help us reduce defense spending from the current annual rate of almost $300 billion to a level nearer $200 billion by 1996. All of the savings should be dedicated to deficit reduction.

(3) Raise the gasoline tax by ninety-five cents a gallon (in addition to the five cents per gallon increase included in the recently passed legislation). Over the next several years, gasoline prices are likely to rise substantially in any case. If the American people are wise, they will pay for this increase in the form of higher taxes, which will bring them many benefits, including lower inflation and interest costs, an improved economy, and strengthened government finances. If not, the increase will go to oil producers, with harmful effects on consumers, the economy, and the federal budget.

The implementation of these policies would be major steps in the direction of achieving a truly balanced budget by 1996. They would restore soundness to the government's finances. They would bring sharply lower interest rates, which would stimulate the general economy. They would mark a return to orthodox economics.

Republicans have a special responsibility in relation to balancing the budget. As the main guardians of the nation's wealth, they should be in the forefront of those restoring soundness to the government's finances. Unfortunately, in the recent past they have embraced the false gospel of economic growth at any price, with disastrous consequences to the nation. In the period 1981-1990, these wrongheaded policies have dissipated an estimated $3,000 billion of the nation's wealth ($2,300 billion real operating budget deficits and $700 billion net sale of U.S. assets to foreigners). This approach has become increasingly counterproductive with the passage of time. In 1990, wealth dissipation reached an estimated $400 billion, while economic growth had slowed to less than $100 billion. In effect, the U.S. was dissipating wealth at the rate of $4 for each $1 of economic growth.

This harmful approach has saddled the nation with government debt exceeding $3,000 billion, which is continuing to grow at the rate of $1 billion a day. It has enriched foreigners at the expense of the American people. It has been accompanied by ideologically motivated tactics that have interfered with realistic budget behavior. It has undermined the government's ability to cope with recession or other adverse developments. It has placed all private wealth in jeopardy. It has shown that growth through wealth dissipation is self-destructive behavior.

In their own self-interest, as well as for the sake of the nation, the constituencies of the Republican Party, particularly the business and financial communities, should take the lead in restoring soundness to the government's finances and orthodoxy to economic policies. Once we approach the budget problem in a pragmatic, non-ideological manner, we can solve it.

It should be emphasized that balancing the budget is not a partisan issue. All Americans, Democrats and Republicans, rich, middle class, and poor, should unite in supporting appropriate policies for balancing the budget. The very survival of our country is at stake.

About the Author

For the past two decades, Ernest J. Oppenheimer has devoted much of his time to independent studies on public policy issues. He has done extensive work on inflation, energy policy, and other topics closely related to the federal budget. He has published six books and several articles. He has expressed his views in letters to presidents, cabinet members, senators, and congressmen. He stepped up his activities during the past several years, when it became increasingly clear to him that the nation's financial condition was being undermined by self-destructive policies. In 1986-87 he prepared a manuscript entitled "Reagan's Disastrous Budget Legacy," which contained many of the ideas presented in Chapter 3 of this book. In 1989, he wrote a study on the budget problems confronting the Bush Administration, which may be considered a forerunner of the present work.

The author sincerely believes that the budget predicament is so dangerous that it involves the very survival of the U.S. as a free and independent nation. To cope with this predicament, he presents realistic solutions that can be achieved once enough people get sufficiently aroused to demand appropriate action by their representatives in government. He hopes that this book will help accomplish this goal.

Prior to his public policy writings, Dr. Oppenheimer did research and consulting work in the investment banking business. He received the doctor of philosophy degree in the social sciences from the University of Chicago. His studies included international relations, economics, political science, history, and social psychology. In connection with his books, he has been interviewd on television and radio talk shows and has lectured to business groups and to university audiences.

Index

Federal debt: 30, 40, 163, 167.

Federal Reserve: 23, 31, 74, 75, 126, 132, 138, 139, 140.

Foreign beneficiaries (of U.S. policies): 69-87.
See also Defense spending, Sale of assets to foreigners, and
Wealth Dissipation.

Foreign trade deficits: 18, 23, 30, 35, 70 (table), 75, 81, 137.

Friedman, Milton: 47.

Gasoline tax: 11, 17, 18, 26, 73, 77, 78, 79, 89, 105-124, 129,
152, 167-8, 169, 174.
   Energy security: 105, 106, 112.
   Environment: 106, 109.
   Interest rates: 106, 107, 112, 118.
   Automobile industry: 107.
   Domestic petroleum industry: 107, 108, 121, 122, 123,
   124, 168.
   Budget : 106.
   Foreign trade: 108.
   Cost per car owner: 109.
   Helping poor to cope: 109.
   Support from influential individuals and publications: 110.
   Contrast with oil import tax: 111.
   Contrast with price increase: 168-9.
   Obstacles: 114, 115, 116, 117, 119, 120, 121, 124.

Growth of economy: 26, 41, 43, 48, 54-5, 76, 83, 96, 132,
134, 139, 140, 171.

Ideological dogmatism: 19, 41, 49, 50-1, 77, 78.

Inflation: 17, 30, 132, 138, 139, 140.

Interest rates
   Balanced budget: 25.
   Budget surplus: 23.
   Government debt: 30.
   Foreign investors: 73.
   Foreign trade: 73.
   Options 1, 2, 3: 138, 139.

Keynes, John Maynard: 25, 29, 30, 46, 50.

179

How to Order Additional Copies of This Book

In times of confusion about public policy, books can serve a valuable function in clarifying the issues and presenting solutions to complex problems. The publisher believes that *Balancing the Federal Budget* falls into this category. To facilitate the widest possible distribution of this book, a number of quantity discounts are available.

1. $20.00 per copy (regular price)
2. $18.00 per copy, minimum purchase ten copies.
3. $15.00 per copy, minimum purchase fifty copies.
4. $12.00 per copy, minimum purchase one hundred copies.

If you want to broaden your perspective on some of the issues discussed in this book, you may also wish to consider purchasing the following books by the same author:

1. *Natural Gas, the Best Energy Choice,* hard cover, $22.50. This book has been favorably received by experts in the gas industry and has been positively reviewed in the *Library Journal,* and *Choice.*

2. *Gasoline Tax Advantages* paperback, $10.00. This pioneering study of the gasoline tax is a forerunner of Chapter 6. It was favorably reviewed in *Booklist* (July 1987).

A COMBINATION SPECIAL for all three books is presented in the Order Form.

Order Form
Books by Ernest J. Oppenheimer, Ph.D.

Balancing the Federal Budget
ISBN-0-9603982-6-0, hard cover, $20.00

_____ copies at $20.00 each $ _____

_____ copies at $18.00 each, $ _____
minimum ten copies

_____ copies at $15.00 each, $ _____
minimum fifty copies

_____ copies at $12.00 each, $ _____
minimum one hundred copies

Natural Gas, the Best Energy Choice
ISBN 0-9603982-7-9, hard cover, $22.50

_____ copies at $22.50 each $ _____

Gasoline Tax Advantages
ISBN 0-9603982-5-2, paperback, $10.00

_____ copies at $10.00 each $ _____

COMBINATION SPECIAL:
one each of the above books,
a $52.50 value, for $40.

_____ sets at $40.00 per set $ _____

Subtotal $ _____

Residents of New York State add sales tax $ _____

Shipping expenses (see next page) $ _____

Total Amount Due $ _____

(Continued on next page)

Shipping expenses: Books will be shipped via UPS or priority mail. The shipping charge is $3.50 for the first book and $1.00 for each additional copy. If you order *Balancing the Federal Budget* by the box of fifty to one destination, the publisher will absorb the shipping costs. For the COMBINATION SPECIAL, the shipping charge is $4.50 per set. These charges are applicable to U.S. and Canadian destinations. For Europe, add $6 for the budget book, $4 for the natural gas book, $3 for the gasoline tax book, and $10 for the combination special. For the Far East, add $8 for the budget book, $6 for the natural gas book, $4 for the gasoline tax book, and $13 for the combination special. These shipments will be made by air.

Please enclose payment with order. Make check payable to Pen & Podium, Inc. Checks from foreign countries should be in U.S. currency, drawn on a bank situated in New York City. Send order to: Pen & Podium, Inc., 40 Central Park South, New York, N.Y. 10019. Telephone: (212) 759-8454.

Please print or type your name and address below:

Name _____

Company _____

Street _____

City, State, Zip _____